"For helping professionals workin
adolescents—those who may be vic
from the home or sex trafficking—C
validated, clinically-sophisticated

implementation instructions) designeu to estabiish rapport, safety and support. The highly ingenious and practical exercises are organized to promote therapeutic growth in three important areas of self-expression, coping and positive thinking, and offer state-of-the-art strategies certain to enable growth, development and a sense of being understood among traumatized clients."

*—Jeanne C. Marsh, PhD, MSW, George Herbert Jones Distinguished Service
Professor, University of Chicago, School of Social Service Administration*

"A must-have for clinicians working with children. Dr. D'Amico has put together a fabulous collection of simple, effective activities with examples. The book is easy to read and should be easy to use! I anticipate using these techniques in practice and sharing the book with fellow practitioners. I am enthusiastic about art and the potential for healing!"

*—Julia Ostendorf, MD, FAAP, 25 years in general
pediatrics practice, clinical instructor PA program*

"As an attorney who regularly works with children in the capacity of a Guardian ad Litem in both juvenile and family law matters, I found this book exceptionally helpful. Oftentimes, and as Dr. D'Amico points out, children who have been through traumatic life experiences are hesitant to open up and discuss these events—especially with a stranger. These exercises are great 'ice breakers' to use in an effort to avoid further traumatizing these children, and instead giving them a safe environment to express their feelings and begin the healing process. I highly recommend this book and plan to use many of these exercises in the near future."

*—Breanne M. Bucher, Attorney at Law, Walden & Schuster, S.C.,
Juvenile Law Section Chair – Waukesha County Bar Association*

"Trauma experienced in childhood or adolescence is a major contributor to the development of a substance use disorder, one of the leading public health problems of today. Through this book, Dr. D'Amico has gifted the world with a treasure trove of developmentally-sensitive, easy-to-use tools for working with severely traumatized children and adolescents to support their healing. Drawing on her decades of clinical experience as well as practical ingenuity, Dr. D'Amico has created a valuable toolbox for youth-serving professionals full of activities that are likely to be enjoyable for both youth and professional, and that can be implemented using common supplies or recycled objects."

*—Sion Kim Harris, PhD, Co-Director, Center for Adolescent Substance Abuse Research,
Boston Children's Hospital, Assistant Professor of Pediatrics, Harvard Medical School*

"Therapists and other healing professionals will find this book to be an invaluable resource for engaging children and adolescents in a hands-on and creative way to nurture a strong therapeutic alliance, enhance emotional processing, and achieve meaningful therapeutic change. These simple yet clinically elegant exercises, through the use of the youth's own internal metaphors, will cultivate increased self-awareness and encourage patients to experiment with different ways of thinking, feeling and being. Through symbolic representation, help your patients overcome blocks caused by cognitive defenses and language traps to keep them moving toward treatment goals of improved self-regulation, coping, and healing. *101 Arts-Based Activities to Get Children and Adolescents Talking* is useful within moments after picking it up, due to the simple, organized way that each exercise is described, followed by a brief case example for use in both a younger and older child."

—*Jenna Saul, MD, DFAACAP, CEDS, Clinical Assistant Professor,*
Medical College of Wisconsin Department of Psychiatry

"I support this book and activities as a way to help vulnerable children cope with trauma and regain lost hope."

—*Estomih Mduma, Haydom Global Health Research Centre*
at Haydom Lutheran Hospital, Manyara, Tanzania

101
Mindful
Arts-Based Activities

TO GET CHILDREN AND ADOLESCENTS
TALKING

of related interest

More Creative Coping Skills for Children
Activities, Games, Stories, and Handouts to Help Children Self-regulate
Bonnie Thomas
ISBN 978 1 78592 021 9
eISBN 978 1 78450 267 6

Creative Coping Skills for Children
Emotional Support through Arts and Crafts Activities
Bonnie Thomas
ISBN 978 1 84310 921 1
eISBN 978 1 84642 954 5

The Big Book of EVEN MORE Therapeutic Activity Ideas for Children and Teens
Inspiring Arts-Based Activities and Character Education Curricula
Lindsey Joiner
ISBN 978 1 84905 749 3
eISBN 978 1 78450 196 9

The Big Book of Therapeutic Activity Ideas for Children and Teens
Inspiring Arts-Based Activities and Character Education Curricula
Lindsey Joiner
ISBN 978 1 84905 865 0
eISBN 978 0 85700 447 5

The Expressive Arts Activity Book
A Resource for Professionals
Suzanne Darley and Wende Heath
Foreword by Gene D. Cohen MD, PhD
ISBN 978 1 84310 861 0
eISBN 978 1 84642 737 4

Focusing and Calming Games for Children
Mindfulness Strategies and Activities to Help Children to Relax, Concentrate and Take Control
Deborah M. Plummer
Illustrated by Jane Serrurier
ISBN 978 1 84905 143 9
eISBN 978 0 85700 344 7

101 Mindful Arts-Based Activities

TO GET CHILDREN AND ADOLESCENTS TALKING

WORKING WITH SEVERE TRAUMA, ABUSE AND NEGLECT USING FOUND AND EVERYDAY OBJECTS

DAWN D'AMICO, LCSW, PhD

Jessica Kingsley *Publishers*
London and Philadelphia

First published in 2017
by Jessica Kingsley Publishers
73 Collier Street
London N1 9BE, UK
and
400 Market Street, Suite 400
Philadelphia, PA 19106, USA

www.jkp.com

Library of Congress Cataloging in Publication Data
Names: D'Amico, Dawn, author.
Title: 101 mindful arts-based activities to get children and adolescents
   talking : working with severe trauma, abuse and neglect using found and
   everyday objects / Dawn D'Amico.
Other titles: Mindful arts-based activities to get children and adolescents
   talking | One hundred and one mindful arts-based activities to get
   children and adolescents talking
Description: London ; Philadelphia : Jessica Kingsley Publishers, 2017.
Identifiers: LCCN 2016038350 | ISBN 9781785927317 (alk. paper)
Subjects: | MESH: Stress Disorders, Traumatic--therapy | Child Abuse--therapy
   | Mindfulness--methods | Art Therapy--methods | Adolescent | Case Reports
Classification: LCC RJ506.P66 | NLM WM 172.5 | DDC 618.92/8521065156-
   -dc23 LC record available at https://lccn.loc.gov/2016038350

British Library Cataloguing in Publication Data
A CIP catalogue record for this book is available from the British Library

ISBN 978 1 78592 731 7
eISBN 978 1 78450 422 9

Printed and bound in Great Britain

I would like my book dedicated to Agatha.

ACKNOWLEDGMENTS

This book is especially for Agatha. And to all of the other children, adolescents and their families, including Jessica and her children, who, like the fabled Phoenix, rose from pain to triumph. Thank you Kay: Your encouragement, clear thinking and support were invaluable. Thank you, Dr. Chandler Screven—in memory, I hope you are proud. This work was also lovingly supported by the ones with four paws: one continuously snoring at my feet, one in my lap at the computer, purring and making edits as she deems necessary, and finally one weaving through my feet. Last but not least, to Lisa, Sarah, Danielle and Alex—thank you for giving me a chance! You have no idea how you change lives. Thank you ALL!

CONTENTS

Part 2

Coping

Part 3

Positive Thinking

PREFACE

As we know, severely traumatized children and adolescents have difficulty opening up, feeling safe and talking about trauma, yet this is our goal. In order to achieve this goal, we need to establish rapport, safety and support so that these children and adolescents can begin to open up and tell their stories. Without their input we cannot help them. Therefore, opening up and the subsequent information gathering is critical. It is the first step in the therapeutic relationship and it is the most difficult step, especially with this population.

The techniques herein will allow the child/adolescent to open up and will allow you to collect the information.

INTRODUCTION

This book is designed to help clinicians, teachers, aid workers and students who are working with children and adolescents aged 5–17 who have experienced serious trauma, such as sexual abuse, physical abuse, removal from the home, child pornography or sex trafficking. There is an assumption that the individuals using this book will have a knowledge and understanding of trauma. Many of these children and adolescents are more closed or withdrawn than children and adolescents who are dealing with less traumatic issues, such as divorce, or adjustment issues, such as moving to a new home. The issue of serious trauma is becoming more prevalent and requires new and progressive techniques, for which traditional therapy and play therapy is less effective.

The new techniques in this book allow children and adolescents who have endured crisis and trauma to open up so that therapy can be initiated and better focused. It is common for a clinician or student to work with children and adolescents whose trauma level is so significant that they cannot talk. They are afraid. They have told so many people already—the first person they talked to for help, police, court systems, family—and now yet another person: you. This is a daunting task for clinicians. The brain does not always recognize the difference between remembering and retelling and actually being there. So it can be indeed a fear-filled, apprehensive undertaking on the part of both parties. As clinicians and students, we never quite know the extent of the abuse that we are about to hear.

I remember in my own practice when I had a case file several inches thick. I knew the situation was grave: several young children, all siblings under the age of ten, had been sexually molested by their 14-year-old brother. It was a difficult situation to work with the children and parents, who were not eating and not sleeping, and who had already told the story to a forensic team, parents, social workers, etc.

How do you start? Where do you start? How do you make this OK for them and for you?

I created the techniques in this book to allow for children and adolescents to be "present" or "mindful" in the moment with me. I used objects with which children and adolescents could easily identify. I did this by utilizing "green" items. These items are timeless and recyclable. Timeless materials are also easy for parents and grandparents to understand and use. Recycling saves on every front.

This book also is designed to help practitioners, who often become discouraged, burned out or reluctant to approach such clients. The fact is, many practitioners are lost within the first five years of working with this population. They are burned out and they leave—not necessarily the profession but this population. The techniques in this book can restore interest and motivation in the clinician and alleviate some of the stress that the clinician feels in these highly emotionally charged sessions.

Who can forget the smell of markers, the feel of glue or paint, the sparkle of glitter? Easy-to-find objects, such as feathers, balloons, shells and paper, create a mini-footprint with a low impact on the environment and are accessible for everyone. That is what you will find here.

This book was developed based on 22 years of work with children and families in a clinical setting. It has been written to provide new techniques, which are much needed as we see a rise in child sexual abuse, child pornography and child sex trafficking, as well as physical abuse and neglect. All case studies in this book are anonymized.

Working with children and adolescents is both an honor and a privilege. True trust comes when parents and caregivers bring us their children and adolescents. To my colleagues and students, here is new help for working with these children and adolescents. The children, adolescents and families we work with have been through a great deal of pain. This book uses recycled and green items to move children and adolescents through pain to a place of healing and growth—to the present, mindful and safe.

USE OF THIS BOOK

This book is developmentally appropriate for children and adolescents aged 5–17.

All tools can be used in both individual and group formats. All tools can be completed in an individual session except Mask of Me × 3, which will take three sessions.

All tools will help children and adolescents to open up and the clinician to gather information.

Many of the children and families that clinicians encounter have experienced multiple traumas. It is with this knowledge that we recognize that some children have gaps in memory due to abuse or neglect. This book contains useful techniques for bridging memory gaps—for example, Green Flash. As children and adolescents begin to tell their stories, a sudden memory may occur or they may share memories they have been carrying with them.

Another example is the Life Story Book. An opportunity to express a life story, even if a child can't remember segments, or has memory gaps, can be thrilling and allow for the building of positive feelings and feelings of safety.

All children and adolescents have a life story, even if a limited one. It is his or her story and should be embraced in the places where it can be supported, and healed in the places where it hurts.

Everyone learns in different ways. As we get to know the children and adolescents we work with, we may find that they learn better using one sense than another. In the different types of activities in this book, using the different senses allows for a fuller and deeper understanding of the concept for the child or adolescent.

Tactile activities are activities that children, adolescents and clinicians use to connect with our sense of touch. We will be using many recycled and found items here.

Visual activities are activities in which children, adolescents and clinicians use sight or illustrations to help convey the message or the skill, such as coping.

 Verbal activities are activities in which children, adolescents and clinicians use only words to convey the message or concept. We do not need any recycled or found items.

Try out different types of activities and determine which is the style the child or adolescent you are working with needs.

This book is easy to use. Simply choose the section you need and choose a technique. You will find directions to implement the technique, including questions that the clinician may ask or that the client or family members may discuss or reflect upon. Each technique is followed by two short examples. The first case sample represents a younger child; the second case sample represents an adolescent.

General art supplies are limited only by your imagination! Have on hand:

- lots of recycled cardboard
- glue
- washable paints
- finger paints
- markers
- glitter
- construction paper
- poster board
- feathers
- beads
- stones
- shells
- pretend "jewels"
- ink pad
- stamp of holding hands or shaking hands
- ribbon
- foil
- list of "feeling words" and emotions or flashcards of same
- stickers of happy, scary or sad faces and stickers of ocean creatures
- everyday objects, such as umbrellas, small mirrors and whistles, also are useful.

Part 1

SELF-EXPRESSION

LIFE STORY BOOK

Purpose

» To share and reinforce positive memories, with the recognition that children and families have limited memories at times due to neglect and abuse.

» To identify people in a child's or adolescent's life, past and present, who have cared for and supported him or her. This tool can also help bridge memory gaps.

What you will need

» Tape recorder and notebook

Activity

Allow the child or adolescent to have a choice between a tape recorder and a notebook for this activity. Let her become familiar with the recorder. Let her learn how to turn it on and off and pause. Do a practice so she can hear her voice and yours. With either option, remind the child that this is HER life story book, so you can begin wherever she would like.

Focus on strengths and key people who care, even if they are not caregivers, such as teachers. Encourage the sharing with open-ended questions.

When traumatic parts of the child's story come up, ask her what she did to get through it, and which things helped her. Ask how she kept it from getting worse.

Case study: **Child**

Melanie, a six-year-old, was referred for treatment. Her teachers noticed her withdrawing and starting to suck her thumb. On one occasion she had a toileting accident at home. The clinician meets with Melanie and explains the technique. Melanie is excited. She first manipulates the recording device, even taking a peek at the mini-cassette, but decides she would rather make a paper book. She reveals she has had a diary in the past. Melanie chooses to color the front page of her book red. She places sticky stars all over it. In her book, Melanie talks about her friends, school and parents. She reveals that her parents are arguing a lot and she becomes frightened and hides under her covers in bed. Sometimes she is so frightened she wets the bed. Melanie reveals that she has told her teacher and her maternal grandmother, both of whom have been supportive. She talks about going to stay with her grandparents on the weekends, which is fun because she helps Grandma make cookies and she and Grandpa build snow forts together.

Melanie was able to overcome her reluctance to engage with the clinician because she loved the idea of making a book. She was familiar with books and diaries and was quite good at reading for her age.

Case study: **Adolescent**

Hannah is a 14-year-old girl who was referred to the office for sexual assault by her brother's best friend, aged 16. The clinician explains the technique to Hannah. Hannah decides to use the recorder. She states that this will be hard, but asks that people only ask her about the incident and not what her life was like before or what she is hoping her life will be like in the future. Hannah begins her story.

Hannah was able to overcome her reluctance to engage with the clinician because the recording device allowed for her to be more open and less embarrassed. At times, she simply closed her eyes and talked.

KEYS

Purpose

» To allow the child or adolescent to open up and be acknowledged, with recognition that what he or she has to say is important. He or she has the keys to communication and, thus, getting help.

What you will need

» Recycled keys of any kind

Activity

Bring out a container of multiple kinds of keys. Discuss with the individual what keys do—they unlock things. They open up doors. Allow the individual to rummage through the container and look at all of the keys. He may be attracted to certain kinds, such as the big, old-fashioned ones.

Once he chooses a key, talk about what kind of door it might open. Maybe it opens a big old door in a house, or maybe it opens a car door, or a barn door, etc. The possibilities are endless. Allow the individual to add ideas.

Begin to discuss the idea that the individual child or adolescent holds the key to his own inner self or world of emotions and feelings and his life story. Talk about the idea of using the key to unlock one story to share for today. It might be a readily known story or a story that has never been told. It is up to the individual.

Case study: **Child**

Shelby is a six-year-old boy who was referred for issues of picking his skin to the point of bleeding, as well as screaming at and kicking his mother. He is also having acting-out behaviors, including biting, at school. He is in the first grade. He is advanced for his grade level.

The clinician explains the Keys tool to Shelby. Shelby has his own set of keys and, in fact, sometimes lets himself into his house after school when Mom is not home. Shelby reveals that he is nervous about being home alone and sometimes goes to a neighbor's house, but his mother told him not to because she could get in trouble.

Immediately, through the use of the Keys tool, Shelby was able to relate and begin to open up. The clinician was able to gather valuable information from the child.

Case study: **Adolescent**

Terrel is a 15-year-old male who was referred for issues of depression and a suicide attempt. He has returned from an inpatient stay and this is his first day of treatment outside of the hospital.

After the clinician explains the Keys tool, Terrel chooses an old key that reminds him of his grandfather. He states that his grandfather had a shed and he would help his grandfather with planting and painting around the home. Grandpa kept many tools in the shed and that is where they would prepare for their projects. Terrel enjoyed working with his grandfather.

Terrel's grandfather passed away almost two years ago and he misses him. Both of his parents are busy professionals who do not have a lot of time for Terrel and his sister.

This opening up and information which Terrel provided allows for the clinician to move forward with their work together.

TIPS FOR CLINICIANS: It has been my experience that when the children and adolescents are empowered through the use of these tools they are motivated to work on bridging memory gaps as well.

MAGNIFYING GLASS

Purpose

» To allow the child or adolescent to open up and take a closer look at what is of concern, worry or fear.

What you will need

» Magnifying glass

» Objects to explore, such as dried seaweed

Activity

Clinicians should have a large magnifying glass available and some objects to explore. Dried seaweed is a good object, as it has imbedded within it other elements, such as rocks, sand and sometimes shells. The clinician shares with the child or adolescent that they will be working on and taking a look at things from a closer perspective today. These can include things inside of us, as well as outside.

Case study: **Child**

Chris is a ten-year-old boy referred for sudden weight loss and fear of going to sleep. Chris has no history of sleep disturbance in the past.

The clinician explains the tool and gives the magnifying glass to Chris to handle. Chris states that it is cool and that he had a very small one when he was little. He shares that he used to collect leaves and bugs and grass and would look at these items through his magnifying glass.

The clinician gives Chris the seaweed to explore. He takes his time and turns it over and over to find little things. He seems to enjoy the experience. The clinician explains that they can also explore closely how Chris is and what he is thinking about or concerned about. Chris acknowledges that he knows why he is in the office and that his parents are worried about him.

Chris begins to cry and states that he has been bullied at school by some of the children. One of the children in particular calls him a pig and states that he is fat. Chris also reveals that he is having nightmares about going to school. One of his nightmares was so dramatic that he does not want to go to sleep for fear of having bad nightmares.

The clinician is now able to move forward to help Chris, after gathering this information.

Case study: **Adolescent**

Gabie is a 14-year-old girl who was referred for issues of defiance with parents and teachers. She was recently given a ticket at school for smoking on campus.

The clinician explains the tool to Gabie. She responds that she is not that interested in science. The clinician says she does not have to look at the seaweed but she can explore something of her own if she wishes. Gabie removes a compact from her purse and takes a cursory glance at the compact. She finds a hair in it and pulls it out. The clinician states that sometimes we might think we know what something is and we find more things than we think are there.

The clinician asks Gabie if there is anything she would like to look closer at regarding her feelings—in particular, about the recent ticket at school for smoking. Gabie acknowledges that she did receive the ticket but adds, "It was lame and stupid because everyone smokes." She went on to say that she is always the one to get caught but that everyone is doing everything at her high school.

This opening up of Gabie allows for the clinician to move forward in helping her.

TIPS FOR CLINICIANS: At times, children, and particularly adolescents, can become quite self-critical. Be watchful of this and guide them in the direction of information gathering rather than criticizing.

FIGHTER FISH

Purpose

» To identify where the child or adolescent has encountered adversity and how he or she has managed it.

What you will need

» Old magazines with photos of fighter fish or similar photos from the Internet

Activity

Have the child or adolescent talk about the concept of a fighter fish. Has she ever seen them in an aquarium? What do they do? Why do they do it?

Fighter fish, like the common Betta fish, are fish that can eat almost anything in their environment. They do this to survive.

What does the child or adolescent think about that? Is it cool? Or is it scary? Have there been times when the child or adolescent felt like she had to attack everything in her environment in order to survive?

Show her some photos of fighter fish. (These can readily be printed off from the Internet.) Have there been times when she's had to survive in her environment? Maybe even by lashing out?

Case study: **Child**

Shana is an eight-year-old who was referred for kicking and screaming in school and in the home. Her mother's boyfriend was recently incarcerated for domestic violence and she sometimes stays with her older sister who is now 19 years old.

The clinician introduces Shana to the idea of the fighter fish. Shana thinks it is cool. She has had a Betta fish in the past, but did not realize there were so many different types of fighting fish. Shana is readily able to relate to the fighter fish. The first instance she describes, however, isn't what the clinician thought would be said. Rather than Shana being the "fighter," she describes witnessing her mother's live-in boyfriend beating her mom. She speaks in detail about the abuse she witnessed. She talks about her mother kicking and screaming and how now she herself is afraid. Shana describes great fear and also reveals embarrassment surrounding her own acting-out issues.

This was a great beginning for the clinician and Shana to be able to start their work together.

Case study: **Adolescent**

Malachi is a 14-year-old male who was referred due to being released from juvenile detention. He has a history of fighting behaviors since age 11. Malachi has either been in group homes, juvenile detention or foster care since age ten. He has not seen his mother since he was nine, as she is incarcerated. He does not know his father.

The clinician introduces Malachi to the concept of the Fighter Fish tool. Malachi can relate. He speaks in slang, discussing how cool it is that fish can fight. He states that he has seen dogs fighting in real life.

Over the course of working on the tool together, the clinician and Malachi discover that Malachi has had to fight for everything, everywhere—even for the essentials like food and blankets.

The clinician now has a good starting place and has established rapport with the adolescent.

WHAT ARE YOU DRAGGING AROUND OR INTO YOUR WORLD?

Purpose

» To collect information on what the child or adolescent is ruminating on or carrying into the present from the past, including images, thoughts and feelings.

What you will need

» An old "Peanuts" cartoon depicting Linus

Activity

Show the child or adolescent cartoons of Linus from the "Peanuts" comic strip starring Charlie Brown. Explain that Linus always carries his dirty blanket with him. Everywhere he goes, the blanket goes, and it affects both Linus and his surroundings because it gets him dirty and it changes the environment as he passes through. Show how this is depicted in the cartoon.

Ask the child or adolescent what kinds of things he carries. Some people carry around mementos from deceased grandparents; others cling to animals, friendship necklaces or bracelets. Some people carry around emotions that influence or change the present. For example, if an individual is carrying around anxiety, fear or low self-worth, even when he is in situations where he can shine or feel good about himself, these emotions may change the emotional environment for him.

Case study: **Child**

Cassandra is a six-year-old girl who was referred for issues of not wanting to go to school and having tantrums in which she would hit her head on the ground—sometimes to the point where it would become bruised. One time it even bled. Cassandra's father recently fatally overdosed.

After the clinician explains the What Are You Dragging Around or into Your World? tool, Cassandra shows a sports bracelet on which is written "We Can Overcome." Cassandra is proud of her bracelet, but at the same time it brings tears. Cassandra reveals that the bracelet was from her deceased father who "was sick." Cassandra knows he took "bad medicine," but doesn't know anything about the drug abuse that eventually led to his fatal overdose.

Cassandra's bracelet represents many things for her, including unfinished business about how her father's death has affected her and those around her.

Case study: **Adolescent**

Rosie, 17, was referred for low self-esteem and a suicide attempt after breaking up with her boyfriend.

As the clinician explains the tool, Rosie completely opens up. She starts to cry and states that she is dragging many things around. She is dragging feelings of low self-worth, such as "there is nothing I can do right," and the belief that no one likes her, including her old friends who liked her when she was with her previous boyfriend.

Rosie reveals that she has had feelings of low self-worth for a long time. It wasn't until she met this boyfriend, who was her first "real" boyfriend, that she felt like she was worth something.

Rosie shares that her mother never really has time for her, and does not invest like other families in Rosie's school events, so Rosie kind of gave up until she met her boyfriend. Now, for Rosie, it seems as if her whole world has changed, including her social relationships with other people, not just her boyfriend. She's begun to feel isolated again and that is what has brought up the feelings of suicidal ideation, which she had in late middle school as well.

Rosie was able to open up and share a great deal of information with the clinician through this tool. They now have a great place from which to proceed.

WISH UPON A STAR 1

Purpose

» To identify the wishes, hopes and dreams of the child and adolescent for him- or herself personally or for his or her family.

What you will need

» Foil

» Recycled cardboard from a pizza container or other box

» Paint, glitter

Activity

Provide the child or adolescent with large cardboard or pre-decorated stars. Some of the stars should be multicolored and include faces. The individual may also choose to make her own star out of cardboard, glitter or even foil. Some children like to draw or color or even paint their stars.

Explain to the individual what the tool is about and get started.

Case study: **Child**

Lincoln is a ten-year-old boy who has lately been tired and sad. His family seems unable to explain why he is feeling this way or why he is becoming more withdrawn.

The clinician explains the Wish Upon a Star 1 tool to Lincoln and presents him with a choice of stars. Lincoln chooses a neon-green star with a funny, joking face on it. Lincoln expresses many wishes, hopes and dreams. One of his wishes is to go to Disney World with his family. Another wish is that he hopes for a puppy. Lincoln also dreams of one day seeing his grandparents more frequently. His grandparents relocated to Florida and they promised him that when he comes to visit, they will take him to Disney World. Lincoln is very close to his grandparents. From kindergarten until last year, he would be dropped off at their home to have dinner with them until his parents could pick him up.

It becomes apparent to the clinician that Lincoln is sad and feeling isolated because he misses his grandparents. They served as his primary caretakers for a period of time and now he does not even see them weekly.

This is a wonderful starting point for transitioning and healing for Lincoln.

Case study: **Adolescent**

Miguel, 16, was referred for fighting in school. He was recently expelled for carrying a knife into the school and threatening another student.

The clinician introduces Miguel to the Wish Upon a Star 1 tool. Miguel states that he has many wishes, but doubts that any of them will ever be fulfilled. The clinician asks if they could work together to put the wishes on a star of his choosing.

Miguel chooses the largest star in neon yellow. He writes quickly with indelible marker: "I wish I was not expelled. I wish I had my girlfriend back. I wish my dad didn't beat me." When he writes "I wish my dad didn't beat me," he pauses and looks at the clinician. He has reached out in that instant for help.

What a wonderful beginning for Miguel.

TIPS FOR CLINICIANS: This tool can be referred to throughout the entire therapeutic relationship as a reinforcement of strength.

I LOVE BEING ME

Purpose

>> To discover what the child loves about himself or herself.

>> To reinforce the positive qualities of the child or adolescent.

What you will need

>> Drawing of a balloon bouquet or a person holding balloons

Activity

Provide the individual with a drawing of a balloon bouquet, or a person holding balloons. Allow the individual to fill in the balloons with words or drawings of the attributes that he likes about himself.

Case study: **Child**

Nine-year-old Brooklyn was referred for issues of biting and picking at her arms and legs and even her toes.

Brooklyn is introduced to the I Love Being Me tool. She enjoys looking at the drawing of the balloons and readily wants to participate. Brooklyn states that she needs more balloons because there are really many things that she likes about herself.

She also discusses the idea that she does not like her older sister, whom Brooklyn refers to as her "adopted sister," previously a foster sister. Brooklyn expresses resentment over her sister. She states that Brooklyn is now getting hand-me-downs from her adopted sister and that her sister is getting all of the attention and "She doesn't even behave!"

It becomes apparent that Brooklyn is proud of her school work, her art work and her friends—all of these were listed in her balloons—and even her flute playing, but feels that none of this seems to matter to her parents. Brooklyn has gone to extreme measures of acting out. It was discovered that Brooklyn is mimicking her adopted sister by biting her own arms.

This led to many good discussions to help Brooklyn.

Case study: **Adolescent**

Pearl is a 15-year-old who was referred for issues of running away and dropping in and out of school. She is currently living with her grandmother.

The clinician explains the tool to Pearl. Pearl scoffs, though she does say that she likes her body and so do the guys. The clinician encourages Pearl to work out some ideas and write them down in the balloons.

Pearl writes down a stunning piece of information. She is pregnant and she is happy about it. Pearl states that she would now be able to live freely and not have to worry about going back to her mom's home. She could stay at the home of her grandmother, who would help her indefinitely. When asked who the baby's father is, Pearl states flippantly that it could be anyone but she thinks it is her mother's 40-year-old boyfriend.

This discussion obviously led to social services becoming involved so that Pearl's health and safety could be secured.

MEMORY CLOCK

Purpose

» To identify memories, both good and bad.

What you will need

» Recycled cardboard

» Spinner

» Markers

Activity

Make a clock, with the numbers representing years of the child's or adolescent's life. Ask the child or adolescent, "What is the most vivid memory for each year?" Compare this with what is the best memory from each year—the most vivid memory may in fact be the best memory.

Case study: **Child**

Mila is an eight-year-old who was referred for being sex-trafficked by her father out of her home. Mila's mother's rights were terminated at age three.

The clinician introduces Mila to the Memory Clock tool. Mila makes a large clock and places numbers in a variety of orders around the clock. She decides to create a clock on both sides of the cardboard—one for good memories and one for bad.

Mila is able to find some good memories up to the age of six when she and her father moved out of her grandmother's home and lived in an apartment. Mila states that she cannot think of any good recent memories until the police came—almost one month ago—to help her.

This was a wonderful opening up and gathering of information for Mila and the clinician.

Case study: **Adolescent**

Luis is a 15-year-old who was referred for numerous issues, including his second suicide attempt, along with depression and anxiety with panic. Luis recently revealed during inpatient treatment that he was allowing an adult male to make pornographic photos of him so that he could make money. He also revealed that he was beginning to like the adult male and felt like he could have a relationship with him. He feels torn because he knows at a deep level that it is not right. Plus, he is fearful for his younger siblings.

The clinician introduces Luis to the Memory Clock tool. Luis creates a small clock out of cardboard. He writes down many positive things about his family and things that they have done over the years. It appears as though things changed for Luis right around the time he immigrated and started high school in the United States.

This is a wonderful beginning on a very difficult topic for Luis and the clinician.

TIPS FOR CLINICIANS: This tool may aid in bridging gaps in memory. Encourage a balance. Most children and adolescents have difficulty shifting from bad to good memories. Allow for this transition and encourage and reinforce them throughout the process.

PIE CHART OF EMOTIONS

Purpose

» To identify how the child or adolescent feels about the present, past and future.

What you will need

» Recycled cardboard or plastic

» Colored pencils

» List of emotions and "feeling words"

Activity

Create three pie charts. Call the three pie charts "Past," "Present" or "Now," and "Future."

Have the child or adolescent divide each pie chart into sections that measure how she feels: happy, scared, etc. The "Future" pie chart should represent what she is hoping for. List her feelings and words. Supplement, if needed, with emotion word lists or flashcards.

Do one pie chart per session and discuss the implications of each one. When all three pie charts are completed, compare and discuss ways of getting to the "Future" pie chart.

Case study: **Child**

Camy is a ten-year-old who was referred for issues of anxiety with panic attacks. Her family members were victims of robbery while in their car in another country. No one was physically hurt.

The clinician introduces Camy to the Pie Chart of Emotions tool. Camy readily completes her "Past" pie chart with feelings of happiness, friendship, love, fun, etc. Camy's "Present" pie chart includes feelings of fear, worry, sadness and physical complaints. Camy has difficulty working on her "Future" pie chart, and the clinician helps her by asking her to identify what she would really like to have more of and less of in her life. Camy states that she wishes her life could be like before the robbery.

This was a wonderful opening up for Camy and the clinician.

Case study: **Adolescent**

Dalton is a 17-year-old who was referred for taking nude photographs of his nine-year-old cousin while she was sleeping.

The clinician explains the Pie Chart of Emotions tool. Dalton completes the "Past" pie chart, which includes emotion words, such as "boredom," "anger" and "frustration." His current pie chart also includes emotion words, such as "fear," "frustration" and "anger." He writes only one word on his "Future" pie chart, and that is "confusion." He admits to the clinician that he feels sexually attracted to his nine-year-old cousin. He is also fearful that he is a pedophile and that he could go to jail.

This was an effective opening up and gathering of information for Dalton and the clinician.

TIPS FOR CLINICIANS: This is a good memory gap tool.

DRAW A BRAIN OR A CIRCLE TO REPRESENT THE HEAD

Purpose
» To identify emotions and "feeling" words.
» To help identify emotions through use of descriptive words.

What you will need
» Recycled cardboard or plastic
» Markers

Activity
Draw the brain or head of the child or adolescent. Have him divide the image into feelings. Discuss: What kinds of feelings are floating around in our heads? Are there many? Any racing thoughts and feelings?

Case study: **Child**

Milo is a ten-year-old boy who was referred after his parents were displaced from their home country. Milo is not sleeping or eating.

The clinician explains the Draw a Brain or a Circle to Represent the Head tool to Milo. Milo draws a stick figure with a very large head. He fills the head with words, such as "alone," "scared" and "sick."

This was a good opening up and collecting of information for the clinician and Milo.

Case study: **Adolescent**

Luna is a 13-year-old who was referred for suicidal ideation after her parents' separation.

The clinician introduces Luna to the Draw a Brain or a Circle to Represent the Head tool. Luna draws a head, which takes up the entire page. She writes many words, including "angry," "frustrated," "sad" and "scared."

This was a wonderful opening up and gathering of information for Luna and the clinician.

FEELINGS WORD GAME 1

Purpose

» To identify current emotions and feelings.

What you will need

» Paper
» Pen or pencil
» Timer

Activity

Have the child or adolescent write down a list of all of the emotions she is feeling or has felt today in a one-minute timed race.

Reinforce the ability to express feelings, even the negative feelings, as it is OK to have feelings. Explore the circumstances and causes of the feelings.

Case study: **Child**

Lucie is an 11-year-old who was referred for eating disorder issues as well as self-harming behaviors.

The clinician introduces Lucie to the Feelings Word Game 1 tool. Lucie creates a list of emotion words, which includes "happy," "sad," "ugly," "fat" and "willful."

This was a great opening up for Lucie and the clinician.

Case study: **Adolescent**

Ezra is a 16-year-old male who was referred for issues of vandalism and threatening others with a knife.

The clinician introduces Ezra to the Feelings Word Game 1 tool. Ezra creates a list of the following words: "ANGRY," "SUCKS," "LITTLE," "RAGE" and "frustrated."

This was a good opening up and collecting of information. Note the capitalized letters that Ezra used for some of his feelings.

HEART NOW

Purpose

» To identify what feelings are "in the heart" now.

What you will need

» Only you

Activity

Work with the child or adolescent by asking, "What does your heart feel like now? Full/empty? Open/closed? Warm, peace-filled? What does it feel like most of the time? If it does not feel open, then try to remember times when your heart felt open. Does that help you to feel your heart more open now?"

Case study: **Child**

Ruby is a ten-year-old who was referred for being subjected to pornography by her older brother.

The clinician introduces Ruby to the Heart Now tool. Ruby describes her heart as feeling hard or even like there is pressure in her heart. She talks about the conflict in her home and that now her older brother can no longer live with the family. She reveals that in some ways she feels responsible.

This was a wonderful opening up and gathering of information for Ruby and the clinician.

Case study: **Adolescent**

Stella is a 14-year-old who was referred for issues of alcohol use and depression. Stella was also found to be attempting to buy alcohol on the Internet.

The clinician explains the Heart Now tool. Stella talks about her heart feeling empty and that many times she feels lonely. She reveals she is often home alone. Her parents are divorced and her mom, who has primary placement, works many hours. Sometimes Mom travels and leaves Stella at home alone.

This was a wonderful opening up and gathering of information for Stella and the clinician.

WHAT COLOR IS YOUR WORLD?

Purpose

> » To identify the child's or adolescent's perception of his or her world through the use of color alone.

What you will need

> » Washable finger paints
> » Recycled cardboard, plastic sheet or paper

Activity

Have the child or adolescent use finger paints to illustrate what his world feels like. Ask him to describe feelings represented through color, such as red = anger, blue = sad, etc.

Case study: **Child**

Sardie is a five-year-old who was referred for sexual abuse by his 16-year-old brother. The clinician introduces Sardie to the What Color is Your World? tool. Sardie likes the idea of painting with finger paints. The clinician and Sardie talk about what the finger paint colors "feel" like and what emotions they represent. Sardie paints a picture using bright yellow and orange. The final painting is one of a sunny day with Sardie, his sister and his parents. His older brother is not included in the painting.

This was a great opening up and gathering of information for Sardie and the clinician.

Case study: **Adolescent**

Wyatt, 12, was referred for issues of homelessness. He, his mom and two siblings were found living in an abandoned car. They now live in a shelter.

Wyatt is introduced to the What Color is Your World? tool. Wyatt laughs at the finger paints and states that he hasn't used them in a long time. He completes a painting that represents a storm. Wyatt states that he feels very confused and hopes that his mom will not be in trouble. He states that he continued to attend school while living in the car and that only one friend knew about his homelessness.

This was a good initial opening up and gathering of information for Wyatt and the clinician.

WHAT COLOR DO YOU FEEL TODAY?

Purpose

» To have the child or adolescent describe how his or her world feels today.

What you will need

» Washable finger paints

» Paints

» Recycled cardboard

Activity

Have the child or adolescent use finger paints or paints to illustrate what her world feels like today. Use colors to represent feelings of happiness, sadness and anger: yellow, blue, red, etc.

Discuss.

Case study: **Child**

Angel is a nine-year-old who was referred after her mom attempted to sex-traffic her.

The clinician introduces Angel to the What Color Do You Feel Today? tool. Angel completes a painting that is purple, black and red. She states that she feels sad and really does not understand what her mother did, other than it was bad. She also reveals that she is angry that no one is talking to her about what happened.

This was a good opening up and gathering of information for Angel and the clinician.

Case study: **Adolescent**

Isaac is a 13-year-old who was referred after his parents discovered sexualized photographs on his phone, which he was sending to other people.

The clinician introduces Isaac to the tool. Isaac completes a painting that represents anger and embarrassment. He states that he and his friends "send photos to each other like this all of the time."

This was a great gathering of information for Isaac and the clinician.

CONFUSION

Purpose

» To open communication.

» To help bridge memory gaps and work toward solutions amid confusion about what is happening in a child or adolescent's life.

What you will need

» Crayons or markers

» Recycled cardboard

Activity

Ask the child or adolescent to draw what confusion looks like.

Ask him to talk about anything he is confused about; for example: why he's in therapy, what's wrong with Mom or Dad, why a divorce is happening, what is meant by depression, etc.

Case study: **Child**

Rachel is an 11-year-old who was referred for issues of fear and anxiety after her mother attempted suicide.

The clinician introduces Rachel to the Confusion tool. Rachel uses markers to draw a face with one eye open and one eye closed. She states that this is how she feels when she is confused. She can look at things, but it looks different depending on how she looks at it. She reveals that she understands her mom was depressed and she is struggling with her suicide attempt and how no one else noticed she was getting that sick.

This was a good opening up and gathering of information for Rachel and the clinician.

Case study: **Adolescent**

Tyler is a 14-year-old who was referred after his father recently disappeared. Tyler has issues of fear and sadness, difficulty sleeping, and not wanting to attend school.

The clinician explains the tool to Tyler. Tyler draws multiple circles in different colors overlapping each other on the cardboard. Tyler states that he feels like he is going around and around in his thoughts. He can't control or stop his thoughts, most of which are terrifying stories of what might have happened to his father.

This was a good opening up and gathering of information for Tyler and the clinician.

PICTURES OF SELF

Purpose

» To identify when and with whom a child or adolescent feels happy, fearful, sad, safe, etc.

What you will need

» Recycled cardboard, ribbons, feathers

» Colored pencils

» Crayons

Activity

Ask the child or adolescent to draw pictures of times she felt happy, fearful, sad, safe, etc.

Have her create only one or two emotion drawings per session. Ribbons and feathers may represent some whimsy or lightness and fun.

After each drawing, discuss its meanings. When all of the drawings are complete, compare and discuss them.

Case study: **Child**

Hadley is a five-year-old who was referred for issues of sadness and sudden onset of enuresis.

The clinician introduces Hadley to the Pictures of Self tool. She is excited and creates a number of drawings. It becomes apparent that one of Hadley's primary caretakers, her mom's boyfriend, is no longer available. In fact, he has recently moved out of the home.

This was a great beginning and gathering of information for Hadley and the clinician.

Case study: **Adolescent**

Quinn is a 12-year-old girl who was referred for issues of alcohol use and self-harming behaviors.

The clinician introduces Quinn to the Pictures of Self tool. Quinn reveals that it feels good to get some of her emotions out. It becomes apparent that Quinn has a good support system, but that she also has significant issues regarding self-esteem and depression.

This was a good opening up and gathering of information for Quinn and the clinician.

UPSIDE, DOWNSIDE, INSIDE, OUTSIDE

Purpose

» To allow the child or adolescent to verbalize unusual, confusing or fearful thoughts or feelings.

What you will need

» Poem below
» Paper and pencil

Activity

Read the poem below and discuss its meaning with the child or adolescent.

> This is confusing—my mind all a wreck.
> I feel lots of feelings—I don't know what to expect.
> Or how to feel—or what do I do?
> Who can help me? Can I trust you?

Ask the child to respond to the poem. Has he felt this way at times? Encourage him to write his own poem.

Case study: **Child**

Paige is a ten-year-old who was referred due to parental abandonment of both her and her siblings. No one currently knows where Paige's parents are.

The clinician introduces Paige to the Upside, Downside, Inside, Outside tool. Paige reveals that she likes poetry and frequently writes her own poems, as well as short stories. Paige proceeds to write her own poem with illustrations. It becomes apparent in Paige's poem that she is experiencing feelings of fear, anger and abandonment.

This was a good beginning and opening up for Paige and the clinician.

Case study: **Adolescent**

Brandon is a 15-year-old who was referred for issues of suicidal ideation. His girlfriend recently broke up with him.

The clinician introduces Brandon to the Upside, Downside, Inside, Outside tool. It becomes readily apparent through Brandon's response that Brandon feels overwhelmed. Not only did his girlfriend break up with him, but he has been experiencing a backlash from her friends as well. Brandon further reveals that, at home, his parents argue and he is worried about his dad's anger. Dad has told Brandon to get over the breakup with his girlfriend, as the relationship was no big deal. Brandon feels hurt, not listened to and rejected by his father.

This was a good opening up for Brandon and the clinician.

BUILDING

Purpose

» To learn what needs to be built or rebuilt within the individual and/or the family.

» To learn what needs to be supported and identifying who is available to help in this process.

What you will need

» Walnut shell

» Paper

» Toothpicks

» Paint

» Markers

» Small piece of clay or plaster

Activity

Have a sample ready of a boat created from a nutshell. Discuss the idea of creativity and thinking outside of the box. Building a boat out of a nutshell can be done and it floats. Hollow out a nutshell and create sails from toothpicks and paper. Install them in the bottom of the hollowed-out nutshell using a piece of clay or plaster.

Discuss the idea of building things in our lives, such as solutions to problems, strengthening ourselves. What needs to be done? Who can help?

Case study: **Child**

Willow is an 11-year-old who was referred for issues of sexual abuse.

The clinician introduces Willow to the Building tool. Willow thinks the boat made out of a nut is amazing. She creates a lovely boat and names it Hope. Willow discusses what the word "hope" means for her. She says she has been feeling "sad and confused lately." She is hoping to get back to her normal self and get through what she needs to do for healing. She reveals that many people have talked to her about what happened and she feels embarrassed and angry that they keep making her revisit her story.

This was a good opening up and gathering of information for Willow and the clinician.

Case study: **Adolescent**

Harrison is a 17-year-old who was referred for attempting to take photographs of his six-year-old sister in various degrees of undress.

The clinician introduces Harrison to the Building tool. Harrison works on his boat and states that he feels now it's not worth working on building anything with his mom and dad. He expresses the thought that his parents are ready to kick him out of the house for what they caught him attempting to do. He does feel that his maternal aunt and uncle are more understanding and his aunt has already reached out to him. He reveals feelings of anger, shame and distress.

This was a good opening up and gathering of information for Harrison and the clinician.

BIRTHDAY CLOCK 1

Purpose

» To gather information about how the child or adolescent felt at special times in his or her life.

» To gather information about how caregivers treated the child or adolescent on his or her special day.

What you will need

» Only you

Activity

Discuss with the child or adolescent different ways people celebrate birthdays. Some families have a birthday party for the individual; some families have a special dinner; and some families have a birthday cake.

Ask the individual what she remembers from the first birthday she can remember and forward.

Case study: **Child**

Olivia is a ten-year-old girl who was referred after she hid in her foster home and her foster parents had to call the police thinking she was missing.

The clinician describes the Birthday Clock 1 tool to Olivia. Olivia is tentative. She states that she used to love birthdays. Her mom and grandma would always have pizza and birthday cake and she would have presents. She says she remembers from her fifth birthday until last year when she was placed in foster care.

Olivia reveals that in foster care she received a cake and presents and that her foster parents and other children in the house were happy for her, but she missed her mom and grandma. She reveals that she hid because she just did not want to be there anymore and was actually thinking of running away.

This was a good opening up for Olivia and the clinician.

Case study: **Adolescent**

Jaden is a 13-year-old adolescent who was referred for issues of depression, anxiety and self-harm. Jaden was also caught drinking from his father's liquor cabinet.

The clinician explains the Birthday Clock 1 tool to Jaden. Jaden responds in an angry way. He states that birthday parties are for babies and that more mature people really don't need birthday parties. They are a waste of money and time!

Afterward, Jaden feels embarrassed and apologizes to the clinician. He reveals to the clinician that at his home his dad does not spend money anymore on anything except alcohol. He states that the last time he had a birthday party was when he was ten and his mom was hit by his father for buying so much for Jaden. Jaden begins to cry. He also states he does not want his dad to get in trouble.

This was a sad, but good, initial opening up for Jaden and the therapist.

BIRTHDAY CLOCK 2

Purpose

» To gather information about incidents that became turning points in the child's or adolescent's life.

What you will need

» Any kind of analog clock

Activity

Show the clock to the child or adolescent and talk about how the clock's hands can be moved forward and backward to set the time. It is surprising how many of today's youth primarily use digital clocks.

Talk about the idea of being able to turn back the hands of time for ourselves. And if we could turn back the hands of time, what age does the individual think he would like to turn back to?

Case study: **Child**

Zoe is an 11-year-old who was referred for issues of grief, which now appear to be depression. She is missing school and does not want to get out of bed.

The clinician introduces Zoe to the Birthday Clock 2 tool. Zoe takes the large, soft children's learning clock and starts to turn the clock hands around and around. She begins to cry. She states that ever since her sister passed away, her birthday does not matter. Her parents don't celebrate and neither does she.

This is a wonderful opening for the clinician and Zoe to begin to explore the issues of grief and depression.

Case study: **Adolescent**

Kinsley is a 17-year-old adolescent who was referred for issues of multiple pregnancies, which have ended in multiple miscarriages or stillbirths.

The clinician introduces Kinsley to the Birthday Clock 2 tool. Kinsley plays with the clock for a while and states she really thinks her own birthdays stopped when she was 12 and became pregnant for the first time. She reveals her parents' anger and outrage over Kinsley's numerous pregnancies.

This opening up was vital to begin to explore the complexity of Kinsley's world.

CLOUDY FACES

Purpose

» To identify what the child or adolescent is currently feeling. This is a particularly useful tool for when children or adolescents are reluctant to talk or are not used to being heard.

What you will need

» A cloudy day and a window

Or

» Google the atmosphere, where you can see live, moving clouds somewhere on Earth

Activity

Look at the clouds outside the window or show the live feed of the clouds. Ask the child or adolescent if she remembers seeing shapes or faces in the clouds. Try to identify together the cloud faces.

The clinician can start by identifying a face and what it looks like in terms of emotion. An example could be identifying a cloud that looks like the face of a woman who is smiling or laughing, etc. Then ask the child or adolescent to try.

Learn from what she says about her own state or the state of emotions around her, such as in her home.

Case study: **Child**

Libby is a six-year-old who was referred for witnessing domestic violence. Her father is currently incarcerated.

The clinician explains to Libby the Cloudy Faces tool. She readily understands and states that she plays it all of the time. In identifying cloud faces, Libby finds many, including angry faces, sad faces, and faces that are yelling.

This was a good initial opening up for Libby.

Case study: **Adolescent**

Mason is a 13-year-old boy who was referred after he was found to be in school with a knife.

The clinician explains the tool to Mason. He states that he is a star gazer and not so much a cloud watcher. Mason likes astronomy and tells the clinician a few facts which he had gathered. Mason states, however, that he is willing to look at the clouds and actually refers the clinician to an online image of the sky.

The clinician shares with Mason what she sees in the cloudy faces, and Mason sees a frowning face. He cannot find other faces in the clouds that are wisping by on the computer screen.

This was a good beginning for Mason and the clinician. The clinician was able to gather information, including some of Mason's strengths.

SUNNY DAY

Purpose

» To gather information and help the child or adolescent open up to what is OK and positive in his or her life right now.

What you will need

» Photographs of sunny days from all around the world or in different types of environments, such as the city and the countryside

» A one-minute timer—use an egg timer or a phone timer

» Paper

» Pencil or pen

Activity

Show the child or adolescent the different sunny scenes. Ask him how he feels when it is bright and sunny outside. What is currently going on in his life which makes him feel bright or sunny? Tell him you will set a timer for one minute and try to create a list.

Case study: **Child**

Madelyn is a seven-year-old who was referred for night terrors and sleep walking.

The clinician introduces Madelyn to the Sunny Day tool. Madelyn can easily identify with it. She also states that she has been to the city a number of times to visit her oldest sister who goes to college there. Madelyn states that a sunny day for her is when her sister comes home and they have time together. Her older sister can drive and she takes her out for ice cream and movies and they have a good time together. She also identifies having sunny days with friends and her mom and dad.

This is a good beginning for the clinician. Madelyn was able to identify positive moments and people in her life.

Case study: **Adolescent**

Damian is a 15-year-old who was referred for issues of depression.

The clinician introduces Damian to the Sunny Day tool. Damian states that it's difficult for him to remember sunny days. They feel like they were a long time ago. Damian continues to examine the photographs of sunny days all over the world and remembers a time with his family on vacation. He and the clinician talk about who was on the vacation and what they did.

This was a good opening up for Damian, who was visibly depressed.

CLOUDY DAY

Purpose

> » To gather information and help the child or adolescent open up to what is difficult in his or her life right now.

What you will need

> » Photographs of cloudy days from all around the world or in different types of environments, such as the city and the countryside

> » A one-minute timer, which could be a phone timer or egg timer

Activity

Show the child or adolescent the different cloudy scenes. Ask her how she feels when it is cloudy out. What is currently going on in her life which makes them cloudy? Tell her you will set a timer for one minute and try to create a list.

Case study: **Child**

Charolette is an eight-year-old who was referred for childhood obesity and diabetes.

The clinician introduces Charolette to the Cloudy Day tool. Charolette can easily identify with it. Charolette states that there are mostly cloudy days in her life. She states that she knows that she is fat and that she has caused her own diabetes—at least that's what her mother told her.

This is a good beginning for the clinician and Charolette.

Case study: **Adolescent**

Aubrey is a 17-year-old who was referred for issues of selling pills at school. She was also drug tested and was positive for opiates.

The clinician introduces Aubrey to the Cloudy Day tool. Aubrey creates a long list of cloudy thoughts and feelings. She states that she does not have enough time to finish, as all of her days are cloudy days.

This was a good opening up for Aubrey and the clinician to begin to tackle Aubrey's issues.

ANIMAL KINGDOM

Purpose

» To identify who or what in the child's or adolescent's environment is safe or not safe.

What you will need

» Photos of the wilderness from recycled magazines. Some examples could be Africa or Alaska, or any place that depicts different kinds of animals, including those that people may have a fear of, such as bears, snakes or lions.

Activity

Show the child or adolescent the photographs of the wilderness. Discuss the various animals and ask which animals are interesting, which animals are scary, etc.

Ask the child or adolescent to think about his own habitat at home, school and the community. Ask him to identify various people and/or places that are interesting or scary.

Case study: **Child**

Braxton is an eight-year-old who was referred for issues of stress and panic. Braxton lives with his mother and sisters in an inner-city neighborhood.

The clinician introduces Braxton to the Animal Kingdom tool. He enjoys the African savanna photos. Braxton is interested in Africa and would like to go to Africa one day. He likes lions and tigers, but is fearful of elephants. The clinician asks about Braxton's own environment. He tells the clinician that he is afraid to go to school because more than one time the teacher has been hurt by a student.

This is a wonderful opening for the clinician and Braxton to explore his fears in his school environment, which also happens to be in the neighborhood where he resides.

Case study: **Adolescent**

Josephine is a 16-year-old who was referred for issues of stress and relocation into a new school.

The clinician meets with Josephine and explains the Animal Kingdom tool. Josephine can relate to this tool. She shares with the clinician that she is very nervous and that she wants to make sure her new school turns out OK for her. She had to leave her last school, last year, because she was being bullied. She expresses intense fear that this will happen again. She also is very stressed by being in a new school during high school where friend groups have already developed and she will have to try to fit in.

This is a wonderful initial opening up for the clinician and Josephine. Josephine revealed the sources of her stress and fear.

WHEN I WAS YOUNG

Purpose

»   To gather information about memories of the child's or adolescent's past.

»   To act as a way to bridge memory gaps.

What you will need

»   Bubbles

»   Multicolored chalk

»   Black construction paper

Activity

Share with the child or adolescent the bubbles and the colored chalk. The clinician can blow bubbles and just create a sense of play or fun. The clinician can also invite the child or adolescent to draw or doodle with the coloured chalks on black paper. The child or adolescent is invited to join in blowing bubbles or drawing. Sometimes she may try both! Ask how old she was when she liked to blow bubbles or write with colored chalk. What else did she like to do when she was young?

Case study: **Child**

Harry is a 12-year-old boy who was referred for oppositional defiant disorder (ODD).

The clinician introduces Harry to the When I Was Young tool. Harry states that he played all of those games when he was a baby. He is no longer a baby and can do what he wants. He firmly states his childhood is over and it stopped when his dad committed suicide. Ever since then, his good memories have stopped. Harry's dad died when Harry was ten years old.

This was a great information-gathering session for the clinician and Harry.

Case study: **Adolescent**

Maya is a 17-year-old adolescent who was referred for issues of drinking and drug usage.

The clinician introduces Maya to the When I Was Young tool. Maya likes to blow the bubbles and then begins to cry. She states that she wishes she could go back to her childhood, when everything was uncomplicated and she did not have to worry about school, friends, boyfriends or getting into college. She reveals this information while hiding behind her hair and coloring with the chalk on the black paper.

Maya revealed many things in this initial appointment, which was a great information-gathering tool for the clinician.

BLUE, YELLOW, PURPLE, RED

Purpose

» To have the child or adolescent identify what emotional state he or she is currently in.

What you will need

» Different objects of different colors, such as buttons, feathers and flowers

Activity

Discuss with the child or adolescent how different colors may represent different emotions. Give him a selection of multicolored objects and time to look through the colors. Ask him to pull out any colors that he feels represent his current state of emotions.

Case study: **Child**

Frank is an 11-year-old who was referred for attention deficit hyperactivity disorder (ADHD) and anxiety.

The clinician explains the Blue, Yellow, Purple, Red tool. Frank spends some time with the construction paper and ends up showing three colors: red, green and blue.

Frank explains that the red is for anger. He knows he has ADHD and so does everyone else in school. It makes him mad that the teacher has mentioned this in front of his peers. He chooses green because he likes nature. He feels good in nature and less nervous or anxious or high-strung. He reports he will frequently walk his dog around the neighborhood and that is relaxing and calming for him. The final color Frank chooses is blue. Blue, for Frank, represents sadness over his continuing struggle with ADHD and anxiety.

Frank revealed a great deal of information to the clinician through the use of this tool.

Case study: **Adolescent**

Whitney is a 17-year-old girl who was referred for issues of anger and threats of suicide.

The clinician introduces Whitney to the concept of the Blue, Yellow, Purple, Red tool. Whitney immediately chooses the colors red, black, brown and yellow.

Whitney explains to the clinician that she has many "down" colors because she feels very sad and angry. Her father's job may move the family right before her senior year in high school. Whitney states there is one ray of hope, the yellow. Her mom and dad are considering letting her live with her aunt, who lives in the same school district in which they currently reside, so that Whitney can complete her senior year. Whitney reveals a great deal about herself and her family circumstances using the Blue, Yellow, Purple, Red tool.

MEMORIES

Purpose

> » To determine which memories are most outstanding in the child's or adolescent's emotional frame of reference.

What you will need

> » Only you

Activity

Discuss the idea of memories. What are the child's or adolescent's memories that she thinks of most frequently?

Case study: **Child**

Makayla is a ten-year-old who was referred for depression.

The clinician introduces Makayla to the concept of the Memories tool. Makayla understands and is able to discuss a particularly haunting memory of her mom being arrested by the police. Makayla remembers this event and frequently thinks about it. This event occurred when she was six years old. Makayla reveals that many of her family members talk about that time and Mom's current incarceration. Makayla states that she wishes her grandmother, with whom she lives, would not badmouth her mom, as Makayla believes her mom is doing the best that she can.

This tool helped Makayla to discuss critical issues surrounding her life experiences.

Case study: **Adolescent**

Owen is a 16-year-old who was referred for body image issues.

The clinician introduces the Memories tool to Owen. Owen reveals that his earliest memory "that really sticks" is seeing his father dressed like a woman for the first time. Owen reveals that his dad is a transgender individual and that Owen feels comfortable with his dad and where he is in his life, but now Owen himself is beginning to wonder about his own sexual orientation.

This was a wonderful tool for gathering information in a short period of time.

THE ELEMENTS

Purpose

» To identify emotions through the use of analogy.

What you will need

» Photos of the elements: fire, wind, rain, earth

Activity

Show the child or adolescent the various photos of the elements.

Describe what the elements mean. There are many meanings, so choose the ones you feel fit the child or adolescent.

Case study: **Child**

Violet is a ten-year-old who was referred for adoption issues.

Violet's father passed away and her mom has remarried and her husband would like to adopt Violet.

The clinician introduces Violet to the tool. Violet understands the tool and is actively engaged in looking at the elements. She is most readily able to identify with rain. She feels rain represents crying and there has been a lot of crying going on in her home. She states that both she and her mother have been crying.

Violet reveals that both she and her mom have been crying about Violet's biological father. It seems as though the planned adoption has highlighted the continued grieving for both mom and child. Violet's father passed away two years ago.

This was a good collecting of information for Violet and the clinician.

Case study: **Adolescent**

Maurice is a 14-year-old who was referred for issues of oppositional defiant disorder (ODD) and vandalism to school property.

The clinician introduces Maurice to the tool. Maurice identifies with fire. He feels angry, and when he feels angry, he also feels powerful.

It is rumored in school that one of the teachers assaulted a student and Maurice knows the student. He is angry with the school for putting the teacher on probation with pay. Maurice is taking his anger out on the school by destroying property. He has also become oppositional with many adults. He explains to the clinician that she is one of the few people who is listening and understands how angry he and other students are.

This was a wonderful opening up and collection of information for the clinician and Maurice. It will have to be reviewed if Maurice has ODD or if he is reacting to the crisis of his friend being assaulted by a trusted adult, a teacher.

WHAT I WANT

Purpose

> »   To identify the child's or adolescent's current wants.

What you will need

> »   Only you

Activity

Talk about wants with the child or adolescent. What are some of the things that he wants in his life? Ask him to list her top three wants.

Talk about the difference between wants and needs.

Case study: **Child**

Amy is a 12-year-old who was referred for issues of body image and anxiety. The clinician explains the What I Want tool. Amy readily understands the tool and lists her top three wants in this order: she wants her parents to stop nagging her; she wants a slimmer body; she wants to have longer hair.

This opening up allowed for a gathering of information for the clinician and Amy.

Case study: **Adolescent**

Daniel is a 15-year-old adolescent who was referred for issues of suicidal ideation, depression and anxiety.

The clinician introduces Daniel to the What I Want tool, and Daniel states the only thing he wants is to feel better. He wants to get rid of the depression. He states he has had depression on and off since he was 11 and he is fearful of it. He further reveals that he has been hospitalized every year since he was 11 and that many of these experiences have been bad ones.

This is an excellent gathering of information and opening up.

WHAT ELSE?

Purpose

» To discover and gather additional information which may not be readily apparent in a crisis situation.

What you will need

» Recycled plastic or cardboard cut in the shape of a large question mark

Activity

Show the child or adolescent the large question mark. Explain that, at times of crisis, sometimes details or even chunks of information may be left out, even if not purposefully. After a period of time, sometimes we can gather a bit more information once things have settled down and we have time to reflect. Continue to discuss the information with the child or adolescent, allowing her to relax and share additional thoughts and feelings.

Case study: **Child**

Josh is a seven-year-old child who was referred for panic and separation anxiety with no apparent background or trauma known to his family or school.

The clinician explains the What Else? tool. Josh holds onto the question mark with a worried expression. He reveals he feels very anxious when his mom leaves and he has suddenly started to have bad dreams about fires and a fire hurting mom or dad. He further reveals he is also worried for his dad. It is learned later that Josh has been exposed to fire safety at school.

This has been a good gathering of information for the clinician and Josh.

Case study: **Adolescent**

Ryan is a 15-year-old adolescent who was referred for cyber-addiction and underage sex.

The clinician introduces Ryan to the What Else? tool. Ryan holds onto the question mark as he states in a weary tone that there is a lot more, but he does not want to get in trouble. Ryan finally reveals to the clinician that he needs help. He was told by a 14-year-old girl that she thinks she is pregnant by him.

This was a great information-gathering tool for both the clinician and Ryan.

A SPECIAL TIME FOR ME

Purpose

» To gather information about how the child or adolescent takes care of him- or herself, including emotionally and physically.

What you will need

» Only you

Activity

Discuss with the child or adolescent what he does for himself: what actions or behaviors he engages in during hectic or chaotic times in the home that allow him to feel good or help him to stay safe and healthy.

Case study: **Child**

Justin is a ten-year-old child who was referred for issues of sadness and sleeplessness.

The clinician introduces Justin to the A Special Time for Me tool. Justin reveals that in his home there is not a lot of time for anyone. His mom and dad are always on the go and everyone is racing places. Justin used to feel as though his sports were fun, but now, it is not that exciting because he and his siblings have to eat dinner as soon as they get home so that everyone can make it to their special games, activities, etc. Justin does find times during all the commotion to read his favorite comics and watch adventure videos, especially with his brother, who is one year younger than him.

This was a good opening up for Justin and the clinician.

Case study: **Adolescent**

Harmony is a 16-year-old adolescent who was referred for anxiety and trichotillomania (compulsively pulling out one's hair). She has been working on these issues for over two years.

The clinician introduces Harmony to the A Special Time for Me tool. Harmony immediately states that she does not have time for herself. She is always anxious about school, even on the weekends. She reveals that she feels intense pressure about school, but she cannot determine the source of this pressure, as both her parents and her teachers have reassured her that all is well. In fact, it appears as though Harmony is a perfectionist and always wants to maintain A grades in her classes. She is also involved in a number of volunteer organizations. She also has the opportunity to graduate early if she wishes.

This was a good opening up and gathering of information for Harmony and the clinician.

CLARIFYING

Purpose

» To sort out or help to determine what are the most critical issues in a complex crisis situation.

What you will need

» Recycled K-cups or other coffee pods, or cardboard toilet paper tubes

» Markers

Activity

Ask the child or adolescent to label with markers the K-cups or the toilet paper tubes with people, places or events that are currently involved in the situation at hand. Also ask her to label other K-cups or toilet paper tubes with any additional issues that she feels is important.

Case study: **Child**

Tucker is an 11-year-old who was referred for exposure to child pornography, as well as molestation by his live-in uncle.

The clinician introduces Tucker to the concept of the Clarifying tool. Tucker readily and silently picks up K-cups and works until he completes 14! Tucker introduces and clarifies many areas where he needs help, safety and information.

This tool was incredibly effective in helping Tucker to open up without having to use many words.

Case study: **Adolescent**

Cecelia is a 17-year-old adolescent who was referred after being released from the hospital. She was abducted by her stepfather, beaten and sexually abused.

The clinician introduces Cecelia to the Clarifying tool. Cecelia sees the K-cups and asks if she could have a cup of coffee. The clinician agrees to give her one, and when she returns with the coffee, Cecelia is already working on the K-cups. She is also crying as she is working.

This was a very good initial opening up and collecting of information for Cecelia and the clinician.

KALEIDOSCOPE

Purpose

» To identify the child's or adolescent's jumble of emotions after being involved in a crisis event.

What you will need

» A kaleidoscope

Activity

Show the child or adolescent a kaleidoscope and discuss how the shapes inside appear to be spinning and tumbling and moving; how one moment, you may see one thing, and the next, you may see another. Use this as an analogy to talk about the tumultuous feelings associated with the traumatic event.

Case study: **Child**

Sasha is an 11-year-old who was referred for issues of anger and physical aggression. Sasha is having supervised visitation with her biological father, who had been incarcerated for possession of child pornography.

The clinician introduces Sasha to the Kaleidoscope tool. Sasha begins to talk while she is looking through the kaleidoscope. Her words come in a rush. She states that she was sickened by her father and does not want to see him. She feels like screaming at him and at people who commit crimes.

This was an incredible beginning and gathering of information for Sasha and the clinician.

Case study: **Adolescent**

Skylar is a 17-year-old who was referred for selling her nude photos on the Internet and drug usage.

The clinician introduces Skylar to the Kaleidoscope tool. Skylar looks through the kaleidoscope and, as she is looking, she talks about her feelings and how she feels just like the tumbling of the kaleidoscope pieces. She states that she was told by her parents and society that she is supposed to make money, and now she is making money for college, and she believes there's nothing wrong with what she is doing. She talks about how when she turns 18 she can do it legally. The emotions she expresses are anger and frustration—both with her parents and "the system."

This was a good opening up and gathering of information for Skylar and the clinician.

TORNADO

Purpose

» To identify and discuss the myriad issues involved in a crisis.

What you will need

» Two plastic liter soda bottles

» Duct tape

Activity

Explain to the child or adolescent how the two of you will create a tornado in a bottle together. Have the child or adolescent fill half of one bottle with water. You can use gathered rainwater or tap water. Ask him to help hold the other bottle in place—spout to spout—while you duct tape them together. When the tape is secure, have him turn the bottle over and watch the tornado beginning.

Talk about how tornadoes pull everything toward them, and at that same time can cause a lot of destruction and harm.

Use this as an analogy to discuss the crisis in the child's or adolescent's life.

Case study: **Child**

Penelope is an 11-year-old who was referred after· her father was convicted of sexually abusing her younger sisters.

The clinician introduces Penelope to the Tornado tool. Penelope helps the clinician to create the tornado out of the bottles. Penelope is readily able to use the tool to launch into her own life issues concerning the crisis in her family.

This was a good gathering of information and opening up for Penelope and the clinician.

Case study: **Adolescent**

Iker is a 15-year-old who was referred for issues of anger, violence and possible vandalism of property at his school.

The clinician introduces Iker to the Tornado tool. Iker helps the clinician to create the tornado. As they watch the tornado, Iker says he knows that many "things get sucked into a tornado." He feels like he and his family have been sucked into trouble because he is the only Hispanic in his school.

This was a wonderful opening up of Iker and gathering of information for the clinician.

Part 2

COPING

UMBRELLA

Purpose

» To allow the child or adolescent to feel protected; to discuss protection.

What you will need

» An umbrella

Activity

Show a colorful, blunt-tip umbrella to the child or adolescent and ask what an umbrella is used for.

After she states that it is used to keep rain off or to cover them from rain, discuss how an umbrella protects us from storms, rain, wind, snow and sometimes even sunshine. Show a picture of when an umbrella is used to protect individuals from rain and even the sun. (These photos are readily available on the Internet.)

Show a picture of when a person's umbrella blows back instead of protecting him or her. Talk about when the child or adolescent has used an umbrella and what it feels like when an umbrella blows back versus when it is providing protection. Maybe some of the feelings could be frustration, anger, fear, etc.

Give the child or adolescent the umbrella to open up and stand or sit under. Talk about times when the child has been in a metaphoric storm and has been protected by an umbrella: Who or what was the umbrella? What was the storm circumstance? Does it continue to exist? Was she ever the umbrella for herself or another person? If the situations continue to exist, discuss them; for example, protecting younger siblings.

Case study: **Child**

A six-year-old boy named Sebastian was referred into the office for issues of being touched by an older child during school. The clinician explains the technique to Sebastian. She brings out a multicolored umbrella. Sebastian is delighted with the umbrella and immediately opens it up and begins to twirl it. Sebastian shares a time when he used his umbrella as an aid to look for worms when it was raining. The clinician asks about individuals in Sebastian's life who protect him and Sebastian responds with many names. When asked specifically about the bullying, he states his parents, teacher, principal and twin sister protect him. He states he has also protected his sister at times and that he is "worried that something bad could happen to her."

Sebastian was able to overcome his reluctance to engage with the clinician and share by utilizing the object of the umbrella, which had multiple positive meanings and memories for him.

Case study: **Adolescent**

Fourteen-year-old Bella was referred for panic attacks. During her freshman year of high school, a teacher molested her.

The clinician explains the technique. Bella begins to cry. She opens the umbrella and holds it over herself, hiding her face. She states it's all so confusing. Her teacher helped her and was her protector in storms but then he also turned out to be someone who hurt her. When she is under the umbrella, she is able to talk more and more about safety and how she was betrayed.

Bella was able to overcome her reluctance to engage with the clinician and share her story by using the umbrella initially as a thing to shelter herself, even from the clinician's gaze, giving her a feeling of protection.

OCEAN

Purpose

» To open a discussion of what is safe in the world and what is dangerous. This tool explores both the client's immediate world as well as the larger world. It allows the child or adolescent to become involved in making his or her own safe "ocean world."

What you will need

» Recycled cardboard or poster board

» Used magazines with photos of the ocean and ocean life

» Ocean stickers

» Paint

Activity

Give the child or adolescent a large poster board or an even larger board or paper which is relatively thick and heavy. Discuss the activity with the individual. Explain that he is able to be as creative as he'd like in creating his own ocean scene. Make available paint as well as stickers and magazine photos depicting ocean animals and plants.

Remind the individual that he is able to use the entire space of the board, so think big and expand and explore the ocean!

For some individuals, it is helpful to supply larger paintbrushes. Many times children and adolescents, as well as adults, find it safer to work on smaller projects, but a larger paintbrush makes it easier for some to begin to use larger paint strokes and create larger objects. Encourage the use of other tools, including fingers!

Encourage fun and creativity in the ocean project. As the project is being worked on, discuss what the individual is placing in the ocean—fish, coral, jellyfish, sharks, etc.—and what they mean. Use this discussion as a metaphor for beautiful things in our own lives as well as scary or dangerous things.

Case study: **Child**

Sylvia is a seven-year-old child. She has been referred for night terrors, as well as incontinence, which has become a new concern. Sylvia has recently been removed from her mother's care and is now living with her estranged maternal grandmother.

The clinician explains the tool to Sylvia and shows her the variety of art supplies that she can use to complete the task. Sylvia is very attracted to the stickers and asks if she can also have one to wear. The clinician allows her to wear one on her shirt. Sylvia enjoys using paint and working on the ocean project. She loves to swirl different paints together. She recognizes how paint colors combine and plays with the paint. She also makes drawings of fish with her fingers.

As the paint is drying, Sylvia chooses the stickers she'd like to place in her ocean. She chooses many. As they wait for the paint to dry, Sylvia and the clinician start to talk about what she thinks the different animals do in the ocean. All children seem to know about sharks, and Sylvia is no exception. She tells the clinician that sharks are bad and that they hurt or kill other animals. She also shows the clinician a sticker of a cute cartoon-like jellyfish, which she states is friendly and happy.

They talk about how the ocean can be similar to our own world where there may be friendly and happy people and also bad people or mean people. Sylvia shares that she has both in her life. She states that her grandma is both happy and mean and that her mom is bad. The clinician asks why she thinks her mom is bad and Sylvia states that Grandma told her that her mom is bad, and that the reason she lives with her grandma is because her mom is bad and can't have children living with her.

Sylvia is upset at this point and starts to cry. She states that she thinks her grandma is bad for saying that about her mom.

This opens up an entire dialog for the clinician and Sylvia to work through.

Case study: **Adolescent**

Marco is a 17-year-old first-generation immigrant. He was referred for anger and violence issues. Marco is living with his parents, but threatens to run away and leave school. Marco is a high school sophomore. He was held back due to truancy issues.

The clinician explains the tool to Marco. At first, Marco does not want to engage, so the clinician shows him an issue of *Natural Geographic* that has stunning pictures of the ocean. Marco states he misses the ocean. With the admission of missing the ocean, the dialog begins.

The clinician asks Marco about that and he explains that, when he lived in Spain, he was able to go snorkeling and diving with his friends whenever he wanted. He loved Spain and states that he hates it here. He wants to go back to his home in Spain. He misses his friends and struggles with "everything" here. Marco draws a picture of Spain and shows the clinician where he lived. He is angry with his parents, and in particular his father, for removing him from his home. He states that his aunts and uncles had told his dad that he could remain in Spain and live with them. He feels that his dad is like a barracuda just going after whatever he wants with no account for how anyone else feels. Dad was offered a job with one of Marco's uncles who lives here, and Dad accepted.

This beginning dialog allowed for the clinician to explore Marco's anger, rage and truancy issues.

SNAIL SHELL

Purpose

» To discover what gets tightly wrapped or hidden deep inside.

What you will need

» Snail shell or shells

Activity

Show the child or adolescent the empty snail shells. Let her hold the shells and look at the intricate design of the shells. Notice how the spiral of the shell wraps tighter and tighter. Use the snail shell as an analogy for what the child or adolescent may be holding onto tightly or deep inside.

Case study: **Child**

Lidia is an 11-year-old who was referred after her adult sister's suicide, which Lidia discovered.

The clinician introduces Lidia to the tool. Lidia likes looking at the snail shell and wonders how the snail could go so deep inside of the shell that people aren't able to see it. The clinician suggests that maybe it's a way for the snail to keep safe from predators.

Lidia is able to use the snail shell as an analogy for herself, in that sometimes she will go deep inside and "hide." The clinician and Lidia talk about what she is hiding from, and she reveals she is mostly hiding from the images of her sister.

This was a very good initial opening up for Lidia and the clinician.

Case study: **Adolescent**

Brantley is a 17-year-old adolescent who was referred for suicidal ideation. He was recently rejected from his first choice for university and he attempted to take his life.

The clinician introduces Brantley to the Snail Shell tool. Brantley understands and uses the analogy that he feels like crawling into a shell now. Not only is he embarrassed about not getting into the school of his choice, but also because his parents have told him he has dishonored his whole family by attempting to commit suicide.

This was a wonderful beginning for the clinician to understand and help Brantley.

TIPS FOR CLINICIANS: This tool sometimes helps to bridge gaps in memory.

SEASHELLS

Purpose

» To become quiet and listen to the inner voice. What is it telling us? What is our body saying? What is our heart telling us?

What you will need

» Large seashells

Activity

Have several shells available, including a conch shell or other large shell in which you can "hear the ocean." Talk about the idea of hearing the ocean in the shell long after it is removed from the ocean. Demonstrate placing the shell to your ear and hearing something. Ask the child or adolescent to take a few deep breaths and listen, then put the conch shell down and simply close his eyes and breathe.

Ask what his inner voice is saying. What is his body saying? What is his heart saying?

Case study: **Child**

Five-year-old Daisy was referred for issues of hitting and biting her adopted sister, aged two. One of the bites was on the child's face and required stitches.

The clinician introduces Daisy to the idea of the shell. She brings out a number of shells for the child to look at, touch and hold. She has shared the idea of hearing the ocean in the conch shell. Together, the child and clinician each hold a conch shell to their ears. The clinician asks Daisy if she can hear anything, and the child nods. She is listening.

The clinician instructs the child to close her eyes—she can keep the conch shell in her lap if she chooses—and just listen to her breathing, in and out, in and out. She asks Daisy what she notices in her body. The child replies that she notices that her stomach feels upset, like butterflies. The clinician reinforces the response and asks if she feels anything else. The child states no, she does not.

The child reveals that she is having a stomach upset, which is a good beginning for the clinician to begin to talk about what may be causing the upset, and eventually get to what is so upsetting about her adopted sister.

Case study: **Adolescent**

A 16-year-old girl, Jenna, was referred for issues of depression, anxiety and panic attacks. She has seen her doctor recently and was diagnosed with diabetes.

The clinician meets with Jenna and explains the Seashells tool. The clinician shows her a box of various large shells. The clinician picks up a conch shell and listens. She offers one to Jenna to listen to as well. The adolescent listens and then follows the directions to close her eyes and breathe in and out and listen within. She reveals to the clinician that her inner voice tells her that she is fearful. She is worried about her diabetes and sometimes she does not feel like herself, either emotionally or physically. Jenna further reveals that she is worried that she could die or go into a diabetic coma, as her mother has told her that unless she takes care of her diabetes this could happen.

The tool has helped Jenna to open up and begin the process of discussing her issues with the clinician.

NERVE

Purpose

» To identify a child's or adolescent's steadiness, courage or sense of purpose when facing a challenging situation.

What you will need

» Only you

Activity

Discuss with the child or adolescent what nerve, confidence or gusto means. Where does she get confidence or nerve from? Who are her role models? Who encourages her? Where does she get her inner gusto? Does she feel she has it?

Case study: **Child**

Jake is a nine-year-old boy who was referred for issues of anger and has recently punched his teacher with a closed fist.

The clinician explains the Nerve tool to Jake. He immediately identifies with it by explaining that he sees it all the time in his superhero comics, videos and games. Jake has learned that when he gets mad he can get things to stop by "shortcutting them." Shortcutting to Jake means yelling or hitting someone. He says that he can get his younger sister to stop whining if he pinches her.

Jake reveals a lot in this session, from talking about superheroes, which whom he identifies and whose anger and violence he emulates, to inappropriate behaviors that he does to his sister, which he thinks are OK. This is a good starting place for further discussion.

Case study: **Adolescent**

Helena is a 17-year-old female who was referred for issues of lack of self-esteem and difficulty with school attendance.

Helena is introduced to the Nerve tool. She states that when she was younger she had a lot of confidence, but ever since attending a large high school in which her graduating class is over 800, she has felt lost. She reveals that when she was in grammar school and middle school, she was outgoing and had many friends. She has a few people now whom she admires and who are her role models, especially her English teacher, who has been praising her and encouraging her to enter her poetry into a competition.

Helena also admires the way this teacher dresses and carries herself. Helena states some of the students make fun of this teacher but Helena gets confidence from her because the teacher supports her and encourages her to continue her writing. Helena also reveals that at times she avoids school because she identifies herself more as a "hippie" than a "preppy" and she feels that her school "is all about preppy." She states it is easier for her to go to school on days when she has her English class or her art class.

This was a good initial opening up and identification of what helps Helena to feel more confident in herself.

TIPS FOR CLINICIANS: This tool can be referred to throughout the entire therapeutic relationship as a reinforcement of strength.

TURNING BACK THE HANDS OF TIME 1

Purpose

» To identify and collect information that has been hurtful or with which the child or adolescent is still struggling, emotionally or physically, or both.

What you will need

» A large clock with movable hands out of soft Styrofoam, or child's learner clock

» Cardboard circle with two clock hands

Activity

Demonstrate to the individual how this type of clock is used to teach young children how to tell time. The soft material is very flexible and so are the clock's arms—they can be moved as fast as the individual wants. Allow the individual to hold the soft clock and look at it.

Give the individual a large, pre-cut white construction paper or cardboard circle. On the circle are two clock hands. Ask him to place numbers along the clock to represent ages corresponding to events. So from the earliest best and worst events, he will place a number to represent each. He can also place a symbol if he chooses, such as an emotion face drawing or sticker.

Allow the child or adolescent to complete the project and then go through his personal clock.

Case study: **Child**

Lindsey is a ten-year-old child who was referred after overdosing on her mother's sleeping pills.

The clinician explains the concept of the Turning Back the Hands of Time 1 tool. Lindsey states this could be difficult and she takes a deep breath before she starts. Lindsey lists many interesting events, such as competing in dance, horseback riding and wall climbing. With the clinician, she identifies other events, such as her parents' divorce, moving to a different home, changing schools and, eventually, her suicide attempt.

This tool gave the clinician and Lindsey a real opportunity to discuss the many things that have been happening in Lindsey's life.

Case study: **Adolescent**

Munroe is a 16-year-old male who has been referred for a history of armed robbery while living in another country.

The clinician reviews the concept of the tool, and before Munroe starts the project, he states that he wishes he could turn back the hands of time. Munroe starts to speak immediately of different times in his life, during which he became involved in gang violence, as young as age nine. He states that he was incarcerated in Peru and that, in Peru, he had to become part of a gang while incarcerated so that he would not be molested by other boys or the guards.

This revelation by Munroe led the therapist and Munroe to begin the healing process from these traumas.

TURNING BACK THE HANDS OF TIME 2

Purpose

> » To find out what the child or adolescent recognizes as his or her best and worst life experiences.

What you will need

> » Play-Doh, or homemade modeling clay that you've made out of flour and water
>
> » Beads
>
> » String

Activity

Allow the child or adolescent to choose which object she would like to manipulate while you talk together. If you have used the Turning Back the Hands of Time 1 tool, remind her of that tool: If we could turn back the clock 24 hours, what were the best and worst thoughts or feelings that she had?

Discuss what were the best times and worst times (situations, events) in her life.

Case study: **Child**

Chloe is a ten-year-old child who was referred for trying to start a fire in her blanket while she was lying under it. Chloe is awaiting inpatient treatment for her psychological state.

The clinician explains the concept of the Turning Back the Hands of Time 2 tool. Chloe also chooses to use a stress ball to roll around and play with as they talk. Chloe seems embarrassed. She states that she wishes that she did not have to go to the hospital. Her parents have told her that she would and that what she did was crazy and that she was behaving in a crazy way.

Chloe took this to mean that maybe she was crazy. She starts to cry and states that she did not mean to do it. She explains that her older brother has a lighter and he is always playing with it and flicking it open to expose the flame. She also states that she is feeling really sad lately and this game she was playing was different and exciting.

This revelation by Chloe allowed for the clinician to gain insight into Chloe's dangerous behaviors.

Case study: **Adolescent**

Jamie is a 15-year-old male who was referred for attacking and breaking his teacher's nose. He is currently suspended from school.

When the clinician meets with Jamie, he states that most days he would like to turn back the hands of time. He adds that, for the most part, most days do not have many good parts to them. If they feel good, it is from doing unacceptable behaviors like punching his teacher.

Jamie regrets punching his teacher—not because he hurt his teacher or even because it was inappropriate behavior—but rather he regrets his behavior because now he will have to miss his friends and girlfriend at school.

This insight provides the clinician with a starting point for working with Jamie.

TIPS FOR CLINICIANS: This tool is useful in bridging memory gaps.

HANDS

Purpose

» To remember good things that individuals do to help themselves and others with their hands.

» To help recall when people have helped us with their hands.

» To help recall when the child or adolescent may have been hurt at other people's hands.

» To help children or adolescents to learn new ways of helping themselves with their hands.

What you will need

» Used cardboard

» Scissors

» Rubber stamp of hands holding each other

» Art supplies, such as glue, glitter, felt, feathers, paint, finger paint, etc.

Activity

Have the child or adolescent trace his hands, then cut out and decorate the tracings. Discuss the tracings, including the following questions, as appropriate:

» What do hands do? Examples to discuss could be: They help us learn math. They help us eat. They help us draw. They help us create art or play music.

» Have other people's hands helped us?

» Have your hands helped other people?

» Sometimes, hands can do things that don't feel good. What do hands do that don't feel good?

» Do our own hands do things that hurt us or don't feel good?

» Do other people's hands do things that hurt us or don't feel good? If so, collect additional information from the child or adolescent, such as who, what, when, etc., in a conversation.

At the completion of the activity, stamp the tracing, using a rubber stamp in the image of hands holding each other. Explain the meaning of the stamp to the individual. One meaning can be that we help each other. Sometimes holding hands can mean support or understanding, or metaphorically pulling someone out of a bad place.

Case study: **Child**

Marlee is a four-year-old child who was referred for reactive detachment disorder. She has been biting, kicking and, most recently, defecating in her bed and placing the excrement on the wall.

The clinician explains the Hands tool to Marlee. She readily wants to have the clinician trace her hands and decorate them. The clinician shows Marlee other children's hands which have been decorated as well. Marlee and the clinician talk about ways that hands are used.

Marlee starts to scream and kick at the table when the clinician and she begin to discuss how hands hurt. It is revealed that someone in Marlee's old home, an orphanage, had hurt her with their hands.

Marlee and the clinician have established a great beginning for working together.

Case study: **Adolescent**

Kincaid is a 14-year-old adolescent who was recently adopted. His name was changed by his adoptive parents. It is known that he was molested multiple times by caregivers in his previous home, including his biological mother.

The clinician introduces Kincaid to the concept of the Hands tool. Kincaid is shy but he complies and traces his own hands. As he does, he begins to cry and talk about how no one until now has ever really cared for him—his hands or anything about him. In fact, he believes that when he wasn't doing "sick" things that his mother wanted him to do, she broke his hand.

Kincaid has a long way to go and this is a great beginning for the clinician and the adolescent.

FULL BODY TRACE 1

Purpose

- » To identify feelings about self.
- » To identify feelings about body.

What you will need

- » Large roll of paper or pieces of cardboard taped together
- » Pen or pencil
- » Art supplies, such as paint, crayons, glue, glitter, feathers, sequins and Band-Aids

Activity

Trace the child's or adolescent's full body and have her decorate it. You can cut out the shape, if the child or adolescent chooses. Talk about the decorations and colors used.

Talk about feelings of self. Talk about feelings of body.

Case study: **Child**

Mila is an eight-year-old who was referred for being sex-trafficked by her father. The clinician introduces Mila to the Full Body Trace 1 tool. Mila likes the idea of having the image of her full body, which she can take home if she chooses. Mila allows the clinician to trace her and she giggles, saying it tickles to be traced.

Mila looks through the many stickers, Band-Aids, etc. She takes the Band-Aid box and places many Band-Aids on her heart, on her arms and shoulders and on her breasts and genital area. She also places sequins in her eyes, and puts some flowers and feathers in her hair.

This was a wonderful opening up and gathering of information for Mila and the clinician to be able to talk about all of the different feelings, both positive and negative, which she was experiencing.

Case study: **Adolescent**

Luis is a 15-year-old who was referred for being the victim of child pornography. In addition, Luis is fearful for his siblings. Yet he is torn, as he feels as if he would like to have a relationship with the perpetrator.

The clinician introduces Luis to the Full Body Trace 1 tool. The clinician traces Luis' body and he smiles, squirms and laughs. Luis is readily able to use the different stickers. He places question marks on his head and a large question mark on his heart, along with a Band-Aid and a heart sticker.

This is a great opening up for Luis, as the clinician and Luis can readily discuss the various meanings which these stickers hold for him.

FULL BODY TRACE 2

Purpose

» To identify children's positive and negative views of themselves.

What you will need

» Large roll of paper or cardboard

» Pen or pencil

» Art supplies, such as paint, crayons, glue, glitter, feathers, sequins and Band-Aid

Activity

Make a full-body outline and divide the body tracing in half with a pencil or pen. Allow the child or adolescent to draw a dividing line, which creates two halves of the outline.

Have the child or adolescent decorate each side of the body, creating positive or negative symbols, or perhaps neutral ones. Discuss each of the child's feelings, whether positive, negative, hurt or neutral.

Case study: **Child**

Dominic is an 11-year-old who was referred for self-harming behaviors and suicidal threats. Dominic was molested by his uncle from the age of five years to the present.

The clinician introduces Dominic to the Full Body Trace 2 tool. Dominic has his outline completed and draws the line dividing the sides. Dominic glues stones and pebbles and uses black and red paint on one side of his body. The other side of his body he leaves blank.

Dominic explains that he feels very heavy and sad and confused about his uncle. He still feels like he misses his uncle and loves him and does not want him to get into trouble. The blank side of the tracing is blank because Dominic doesn't know what to feel and sometimes he states that he has no feelings at all, but at times feels numb.

This was a good opening up and gathering of information for Dominic and the clinician.

Case study: **Adolescent**

Mimi is a 15-year-old who was referred for selling photos of herself and selling her used underwear and socks on the Internet to adult males for a profit.

The clinician introduces Mimi to the Full Body Trace 2 tool. Mimi likes the concept and uses glitter, stars and flowers to decorate one side of the outline. The other side of the outline she decorates with flowers, glitter and stars all over again, except in the head. There, she uses thunderbolts and draws exclamation marks.

Mimi explains to the clinician that she is mad at her parents. She knows many girls who are doing what she's doing on the Internet and feels as though there is nothing wrong with it. She states she uses a different name and that she is paid via gift cards and that no one is hurt. She insists that her parents are awful and abusive and want her to make money babysitting and doing other miscellaneous jobs, when she can make so much money she could pay for her own college. She reveals that she intends to continue her behaviors.

This was an excellent opening up and gathering of information for Mimi and the therapist.

FEELINGS WORD GAME 2

Purpose

- » To identify emotions.
- » To reinforce the use of words in expressing feelings.
- » To provide an increase in the range of words used to describe feelings.

What you will need

- » Paper
- » Pen or pencil
- » Timer

Activity

Have the child or adolescent write down a list of all of the emotions he can think of in a one-minute timed race.

Reinforce the ability to express feelings, even the negative feelings, as it is OK to have our feelings.

Talk about other words that could be used.

Case study: **Child**

Hazel is a five-year-old who was referred for adjustment disorder issues in her new home and school.

The clinician introduces Hazel to the Feelings Word Game 2 tool. Together, Hazel and the clinician decide that Hazel will tell the clinician the words, and the clinician will write the words down for Hazel.

Hazel dictates: "happy," "sad," "scared" and "not sure."

This was a good opening up and gathering of information with a small child.

Case study: **Adolescent**

August is a 17-year-old who was referred for truancy and for failing three out of six classes.

The clinician explains the Feelings Word Game 2 tool. August creates the following list: "depressed," "unmotivated," "frustrated," "hungry," "sad" and "lonely."

This was a good opening up and gathering of information for August and the clinician.

OPEN AND CLOSED

Purpose

» To assess the child's or adolescent's need for feeling closed off or protecting self, as well as his or her ability to be open and feel safe.

What you will need

» Only you

Activity

Demonstrate to the child or adolescent the following:

» Close your hand into a fist.

» Open your hand.

What does each movement feel like? Which feels better? Why?

Then, have the child or adolescent lay on the floor and curl up tight in a ball (the clinician can demonstrate this before the individual tries).

» Uncurl. Uncurl more. Open the body slowly with legs and arms spread like Superwoman or Superman.

» How do these movements feel? Discuss.

Case study: **Child**

Jaxon is a six-year-old who was referred for physical child abuse. The clinician introduces Jaxon to the Open and Closed tool. They work together, opening and closing their hands. Then they move onto the floor and follow the Open and Closed tool. Jaxon finds it difficult to stay open—he feels safer in a ball.

This was a dramatic gathering of information for Jaxon and the clinician.

Case study: **Adolescent**

Finn is a 15-year-old who was referred for depression. Finn has been hospitalized three times for this issue.

The clinician introduces Finn to the Open and Closed tool. Finn likes the idea of doing the movements on the floor. He reveals that, on many days, he stays in his bed, closed and rolled up like a ball, sometimes even with the blanket over his head. He states he prefers this to other activities.

This also was a dramatic opening up and gathering of information for Finn and the clinician.

COMFORT/SOOTHE

Purpose

> » To identify what/who gives the child or adolescent comfort.
>
> » To identify what circumstances and environments are safe and comforting.
>
> » To reinforce self-comforting/soothing.

What you will need

> » Only you

Activity

Discuss with the child or adolescent what feels comforting for her, such as a particular toy or a pet.

Give examples from other children or adolescents or self-disclose when you feel comfort. What are the circumstances? Be descriptive. What does it feel like in your body—for example, quiet, full heart, quiet mind, loved?

Explore: people, pets, friendships, etc.

Reinforce how she self-comforts and soothes.

Case study: **Child**

Elliot is a seven-year-old who was referred for panic after he was hit by a car while riding his bike.

The clinician introduces Elliot to the Comfort/Soothe tool. Elliot talks about many things that have comforted him, specifically surrounding physical pain, on which he is quite focused. He talks about his mother rubbing his hands or massaging his temples, which is very comforting. He also talks about playing board games with his older brother, which is also comforting. He also reveals he has ongoing pain and will require a second surgery. He feels fearful and worried that he will have more pain.

This was a good opening up and gathering of information for Elliot and the clinician.

Case study: **Adolescent**

Landon is a 16-year-old who was referred after an injury on his high school football team, which requires both knee and shoulder surgery. Landon will have eight months of recovery, which will require him to have a homebound schooling program.

The clinician introduces Landon to the Comfort/Soothe tool. Landon talks about his girlfriend and how she has been talking with him and figuring out ways that they can still do things together and maybe even attend the prom, even though he won't be able to dance. Landon also discusses how listening to his music helps to soothe him. Lately he reports not being able to sleep well due to pain and worrying about his surgeries and he found a way to comfort himself by falling asleep to movies or stories on YouTube.

This was a good opening up and gathering of information for Landon and the clinician.

SAFE AND UNSAFE

Purpose

» To identify areas in the community where the child or adolescent may feel unsafe.

What you will need

» Community play set or map, which shows roads, railroads, parks, houses, etc.

» Stickers of happy, scary or sad faces

» Pencils or crayons

Activity

Help the child or adolescent personalize the map or play set by adding figures or by drawing on the map. Use stickers of happy, scary or sad faces to add to the map.

Which places/areas are safe and which are not? Discuss.

Case study: **Child**

Cooper is a seven-year-old boy who was referred after he was placed with his maternal grandmother, as his parents were incarcerated for selling drugs from their home.

The clinician introduces Cooper to the Safe and Unsafe tool. Cooper and the clinician use a recycled poster board to draw buildings that represent where Cooper lives. Cooper shows safe places by placing a star wherever he feels safe. He feels safe at home in his grandmother's house and in his cousin's home, a few houses away from his grandmother's home. Cooper reveals that he does not feel safe in other places yet because he does not know his grandmother's neighborhood and he's been feeling fearful since his parents were taken away.

This was a good initial opening up and gathering of information for Cooper and the clinician.

Case study: **Adolescent**

Rita Mary is a 16-year-old who was referred for issues related to rape.

The clinician introduces Rita Mary to the Safe and Unsafe tool. She states that the tool is very difficult for her as she really only feels safe at home. She places two stickers on her home to represent both sad and happy. She states that sometimes she does not feel safe at home. She reveals that she was raped while walking through the park on the way to school. The perpetrator has never been caught. She places sad faces all over the park and the path that she took back home.

This was a good opening up and gathering of information for Rita Mary and the clinician.

WHEN DO YOU FEEL LIKE A LION?

Purpose

» To identify feelings of strength and fearlessness, as well as softness, vulnerability and associated behaviors with which children or adolescents can identify, such as a bird flying away from danger.

What you will need

» Only you

Activity

Discuss the following ideas and questions with the child or adolescent:

» When do you feel like a lion?

» When do you feel like a kitten?

Discuss with him what lions are like and what kittens are like, using "feelings words."

Ask the young person to identify when he feels like these types of animals or others, such as the bird previously mentioned.

Discuss.

Case study: **Child**

Adelaide is a five-year-old who was referred while in foster care for biting her foster sister.

The clinician introduces Adelaide to the When Do You Feel Like a Lion? tool. Adelaide loves the question and she roars. She states that she feels like a lion most of the time. When asked when she feels like a kitten, she quiets down and makes a purring noise. Adelaide states she feels like a kitten when she is with her grandmother. She likes her grandmother's stories and the foods she makes for Adelaide.

This was a good opening up and gathering of information for Adelaide and the clinician.

Case study: **Adolescent**

Iris is a 14-year-old who was referred for underage driving with underage passengers in the vehicle.

The clinician introduces Adelaide to the When Do You Feel Like a Lion? tool. Iris states that she doesn't feel very strong or confident. She usually feels weak like a kitten. She further reveals that the behavior of stealing her parents' car was an attempt to show off or look brave to her friends.

This was a good opening up and gathering of information for Adelaide and the clinician.

PILLOW/BLANKET—SOFT/COZY

Purpose

» To help the child or adolescent to identify things which make him or her feel safe and cozy.

» To remember safe times and cozy times and to facilitate those memories.

What you will need

» Pillow

» Blanket

Activity

Give the child or adolescent a soft blanket. Allow her to feel the blanket or choose to wrap herself in it. Also give her a pillow. The individual can lie down if she chooses or just hold the pillow.

Talk about times when she feels comfy, cozy and safe.

Facilitate and reinforce the positive memories.

Case study: **Child**

Molly is a ten-year-old who was referred for issues of panic, anxiety and night terrors. Her family had recently been involved in a home fire in which no one was hurt.

The clinician introduces Molly to the Pillow/Blanket—Soft/Cozy tool. Molly talks about many memories in her old home. She is currently living in a motel with her family until her home can be restored. She talks about her favorite blanket, in which she would snuggle with her sister or her dog. She talks about many things being missing, but knows that even though her family is not home, they will be soon, and her mom has told her they will restore many things. She looks forward to being able to sleep in her own room and eat in her own kitchen. She remembers that the order in their old home was comforting and felt safe. She reveals that where the family is now has many new sounds and smells and is way too small.

This was a good opening up and gathering of information for Molly and the clinician.

Case study: **Adolescent**

Eloise is a 13-year-old who was referred after being treated for hearing voices. The clinician introduces Eloise to the Pillow/Blanket—Soft/Cozy tool. Eloise talks about many times before her hospitalization that were cozy or comforting, such as watching TV with her parents or playing videos with her brother or sister. She has also enjoyed sleepovers and making a tent in her room where she and her friends can stay. Eloise is looking forward to continuing to have the same comforts. She also reveals that she finds her medication comforting because she "never wants to go back there again," referring to her hospital stay.

This was a good opening up and gathering of information for Eloise and the clinician.

STONE—BUMPY/ROUGH

Purpose

> » To help the child or adolescent to identify when things have been "rough or bumpy," either emotionally or physically, in his or her life.

What you will need

> » Small rough stone
>
> » Larger, heavier rough stone

Activity

Give the child or adolescent the small rough stone and then another one that is larger, rougher and heavier.

Talk about rough or "heavy" times. Talk about how he got through those times and how things did not get worse. Ask: Are there any rough times now?

Reinforce the use of solutions that worked in the past and brainstorm new solutions together.

Case study: **Child**

Lillian is a ten-year-old girl who was referred for neglect by her current caregiver, who is her biological aunt.

The clinician introduces Lillian to the Stone—Bumpy/Rough tool. Lillian holds onto a small rough stone. She describes many rough or difficult times in her life, including when her mom could no longer take care of her due to the mother's mental health issues, and her subsequent move to her aunt's home. She believes that she was better taken care of with her mom and wishes her mom could be better so that they could be together again.

This was a wonderful beginning and opening up for Lillian and the clinician.

Case study: **Adolescent**

Michael is a 17-year-old who was referred for truancy and fighting behaviors. He is currently on probation from school.

The clinician introduces Michael to the Stone—Bumpy/Rough tool. Michael picks up the heavy stone and states that he feels heavy. He feels like he is dragging himself around all of the time. He also reveals that the only time he feels like he has energy is when he is fighting or in a dispute with someone.

This was a wonderful opening up and gathering of information for Michael and the clinician.

TIPS FOR CLINICIANS: Reinforce with the child or adolescent that together you are working toward solutions, so that the individual is able to leave with hope.

ROUGH

Purpose

» To determine what are some of the more difficult or "rough times" in a child or adolescent's life.

What you will need

» Sandpaper and/or rough stone
» Smooth stone

Activity

Give the child or adolescent the opportunity to feel all of the objects and describe what they feel like. Discuss the analogy to our own lives where we may have had smooth or easy times and also rough or difficult times.

Ask the child or adolescent to talk about those times. What has been the most difficult or rough time recently?

Case study: **Child**

Sam is an 11-year-old who was referred for issues of reactive attachment disorder.

The clinician introduces Sam to the Rough tool. Sam feels the sandpaper and the rough stone, and then touches the smooth stone. He ends up holding on to the smooth stone as he reveals jealousy issues he feels when his father pays more attention to his other siblings. He also talks about missing his father due to the father's work trips.

This was a good opening up and gathering of information for Sam and the clinician.

Case study: **Adolescent**

Gianna is a 16-year-old who was referred for testing positive for HIV/AIDS.

The clinician introduces Gianna to the Rough tool. Gianna states that, up until the present, her life had been fun. She reveals she did not have many rough times. She also reveals she does not know how she contracted HIV/AIDS, as she has always used protection. She wonders if her mother was positive for HIV/AIDS and passed it on to her during birth.

This was a wonderful beginning and gathering of information for Gianna and the clinician.

SAFE

Purpose

> » To discuss what safety means and where the child or adolescent feels safe.

What you will need

> » Only you

Activity

Have the child or adolescent give examples of safety, such as holding Mom's hand, being at Grandma's, hanging out with peers, etc.

Ask the child or adolescent to give examples of places where he feels safe or has felt safe.

Facilitate discussion of positive memories of being safe.

Case study: **Child**

Carson is an eight-year-old boy who was referred after witnessing his mother being set on fire by his father.

The clinician introduces Carson to the Safe tool. Carson states that he does not feel safe. He cries and talks about what happened with his mother. The clinician and Carson are able to identify his grandparents as people with whom he feels safe. He also feels safe at school with his teachers.

This was a good opening up for Carson and the clinician.

Case study: **Adolescent**

Tessa is a 16-year-old who was referred due to issues of running away and defiance. She is now living in a halfway house.

The clinician introduces Tessa to the Safe tool. Tessa feels that very few places exist where she feels safe. She feels safe with friends, but only at certain times. She never feels safe at home. She states that she has been running away from home since her father broke her mother's jaw, an event which Tessa witnessed at age 13. Tessa also revealed that she has been trying to get her mom to be safe as well.

This was an important opening up and gathering of information for Tessa and the clinician.

INSIDE

Purpose

» To identify feelings inside of one's body and how emotions affect physiology.

What you will need

» Photographs of sunshine and butterflies from a recycled magazine or the Internet

Activity

Ask the child or adolescent what it feels like inside of her body. Explain that sometimes we may feel butterflies in our stomach, or headaches, or we may feel happy like sunshine, etc.

Discuss under what circumstances these feelings occur.

Case study: **Child**

Nevaeh is a five-year-old who was referred for feelings of nausea and fear of attending school. She has recently begun to throw tantrums when she has to leave for school.

The clinician introduces Nevaeh to the Inside tool. Nevaeh and the clinician look through the photographs of butterflies and sunshine. Nevaeh talks about how at times she feels butterflies in her stomach. Nevaeh and the clinician discover that she only feels the butterflies when she is going to school. Once she is in school they disappear. Nevaeh reveals that at times the feeling is so intense she feels like throwing up.

This was a good beginning and opening up for the clinician and Nevaeh.

Case study: **Adolescent**

Sally is a 16-year-old who was referred for issues of anxiety with panic. She has lost a significant amount of weight in the past month.

The clinician introduces Sally to the Inside tool. Sally reveals that she has felt very anxious lately. She states she has butterflies in her stomach all of the time and actually recognizes that her gagging reflex has been activated. In addition, she states that she has lost her appetite. Sally, who is an A student, has suddenly felt overwhelmed by school and thoughts of college. She feels fearful and feels panicky at times.

This was a good opening up and gathering of information for Sally and the clinician.

SLAY YOUR DRAGON

Purpose

» To identify what situations and people cause distress in the child's or adolescent's life.

What you will need

» Drawing or figure of a dragon

Activity

Show the child or adolescent an image of a dragon slaying an evil monster. (I actually have a hand-drawn one from a young child who depicted a dragon slaying his parents' arguments.)

Ask the child or adolescent what he would like to slay.

Case study: **Child**

Timothy is a six-year-old boy. His was referred for kicking and hitting, first his siblings, and now students at school.

The clinician asks Timothy, "What would you like to draw today that represents how you feel?" In response, he draws a dragon breathing on an argument that his parents were having.

Timothy reveals that his parents always yell and scream at each other. His little sister, who is three, hides under or beside Timothy. His younger brother, who is five, sometimes begins to cry. Timothy also states he feels fearful when the yelling starts. He knows his parents wouldn't hurt each other but he still feels frightened.

Case study: **Adolescent**

Elsie is a 15-year-old girl who was referred for ongoing issues of depression and cutting.

The clinician discusses the Slay Your Dragon tool and Elsie states that she has so many dragons to slay. The clinician asks if she would like some time to write them down or if she would just like to talk about the top one or two things that are concerning her.

Elsie decides she will talk about the main issue that is concerning her now and impacting her depression and probably one of the major reasons she is cutting. She also decides that she will work at home on her list of what else she needs to "slay." She says the list is long and she is worried about this. The clinician reassures Elsie that they will go at a pace that is right for her.

Elsie immediately opened up using this tool and was able to articulate what it meant for her.

TIPS FOR CLINICIANS: This tool is about personal power. Reinforce the individual's ability to create solutions.

ORANGE CONE

Purpose

» To help children and adolescents recognize and identify internal cues that tell them something is not right.

What you will need

» One orange safety cone, or make an orange cone out of a paper towel tube and papier mâché that is colored or painted bright orange

Activity

Show the child or adolescent the orange safety cone and discuss what it means. The meaning of the orange safety cone is to tread cautiously. You could also show an image of an orange safety cone on a sidewalk directing walkers around a hole in the pavement or around a construction site.

Allow the child or adolescent to hold the orange cone. Ask about what is currently going on in her life that requires her to be careful or tread lightly.

Case study: **Child**

Misha is an eight-year-old boy who was referred because he is fearful of his brother. The brother recently used scissors to cut up his own card collection, as well as Misha's. He also threatened to cut Misha.

The clinician introduces Misha to the Orange Cone tool. Misha understands the concept and expresses the idea that there should be orange cones placed all around his brother everywhere he goes.

This was a wonderful opening up for Misha and the clinician to use for further discussion.

Case study: **Adolescent**

Matty is a 13-year-old girl who has been referred for school avoidance and panic when she has to go to school. Matty is no longer able to ride the bus. A parent has to drive her and pick her up from school when she is able to attend.

The clinician explains the Orange Cone tool to Matty. Matty identifies with it and states that at school there is one girl in particular who is bullying her. Matty goes on to identify several incidents of bullying at school, as well as on the bus. She explains that she actually has eaten her lunch in a bathroom stall in order to avoid the bully.

This tool allowed Matty to open up and reveal many issues to the clinician.

CONTAINER

Purpose

- » To organize thoughts and emotions.
- » To help with memory gaps.

What you will need

- » Bottle filled with water or juice
- » Cereal box or jewelry box
- » Silverware container

Activity

Show the child or adolescent the various containers listed above.

Discuss why we contain things: to protect them, organize them or keep them in place. Food is protected in containers or boxes. Silverware is organized to keep for ready usage and to keep in place. Discuss how certain things have certain places. For example, a knife won't fit in the teaspoon area. Or we may have special containers for liquids and solids.

Use the metaphor of the containers to explain how we might bottle up or contain our emotions at times to protect ourselves, or even to help organize our emotions by meaning.

Case study: **Child**

Miles is an 11-year-old who was referred for issues of anxiety and obsessive compulsive disorder. He is not able to be in the same room with "contaminated" things or people, including his mother.

The clinician discusses the Container tool with Miles, who states that he can understand using containers to protect things. He states that he has to protect his things from his mother. He does not want her to touch his things, not even his food or himself.

This was a great opening up for the clinician and Miles.

Case study: **Adolescent**

Nathan is a 14-year-old male who was referred for sudden outbursts of rage which culminated in him punching his father.

The clinician explains the Container tool. Nathan identifies with the idea of protection. He also states that he feels "very bottled up." When he starts to feel bottled up, he feels like he is internally under pressure, like a soda can that has been shaken and then when opened it sprays out.

This is a wonderful opening up and gathering of information for Nathan and the clinician.

TIGHTROPE WALKER 1

Purpose

» To help the child or adolescent achieve balance and open up to share competing issues that the child or adolescent is currently working on.

What you will need

» A photograph of a person walking a tightrope. There are some famous tightrope walkers, like the Wallenda family, and photos of them can easily be found on the Internet or in the library.

Activity

Show the child or adolescent the photographs of a tightrope walker.

Discuss how precarious tightrope walking is and how one must keep balance. The tightrope walker can be pulled in a variety of directions: left, right, and even down. Use this as an analogy to determine what issues are pulling at the individual child or adolescent.

Case study: **Child**

Lauren is a nine-year-old girl who was referred for stress and cyber-addiction. Her parents report she cannot get off social media and will have a tantrum when asked to do so.

The clinician introduces Lauren to the concept of the Tightrope Walker 1 tool. Lauren relates to it and states that she is pulled all of the time. Many of her friends, including someone whom she identifies as her nine-year-old boyfriend, are always on social media. If she is not online, she feels stressed out and that she's missing what her friends are doing. By the time she gets to school the next day, she may have missed a lot. Some of her friends form alliances at night, and if you are not part of it, you may be excluded the next day. It seems that the "group" the next day is the group that stays up the latest on social media. Lauren reports that some of her friends are on it until 1 a.m. and then on again at 5 a.m.

This was a wonderful opening up for the clinician and Lauren. It also reminds us of the use and misuse of social media.

Case study: **Adolescent**

Ivy is a 14-year-old girl who suffers from eating disorder issues.

The clinician introduces Ivy to the concept of the Tightrope Walker 1 tool. Ivy immediately understands the idea. She feels like she is constantly walking a tightrope between eating, not eating, exercising and purging. She states that she has fallen off the tightrope many times. The most recent time is when her parents caught her on a website promoting eating disorders.

This was a good opening up and collecting of information for the clinician and Ivy.

TIGHTROPE WALKER 2

Purpose

» To understand who or what allows the child or adolescent to maintain balance and move forward toward his or her goals.

What you will need

» A photograph of a person walking a tightrope. There are some famous tightrope walkers, like the Wallenda family, and photos of them can easily be found on the Internet or in the library.

Activity

Show the child or adolescent photographs of tightrope walkers, including the famous Wallendas. Discuss how the tightrope walker wears special shoes and uses a pole for balance.

Ask the child or adolescent what or who helps him maintain his balance so that he can move forward toward his goals.

Case study: **Child**

Easton is an eight-year-old boy who is experiencing panic after his family encountered a storm while on vacation and their camper was struck by lightning while they were in it. No one was hurt; however, Easton now experiences panic whenever he hears that a storm may be coming or even when it starts to rain or look cloudy.

The clinician explains the concept of the Tightrope Walker 2 tool to Easton. Easton understands the analogy and states he loves to go on vacation with his family. He shares that he watches his two older brothers and observes how they are OK in the camper and actually having fun. Easton states that the more time he spends with his brothers in the camper, the less fearful he feels.

This was a wonderful opening up and gathering of information for the clinician and Easton.

Case study: **Adolescent**

Xander is a 17-year-old who was referred for stress. Xander resides with his mom and grandmother and six siblings. He attends an alternative school, which allows him to be streamlined into a local technical college when he graduates.

The clinician introduces Xander to the Tightrope Walker 2 tool. Xander understands the concept and says his biggest supports and allies are his mom and grandmother. He states that, every day, he observes his mom and grandmother taking care of him and his siblings and he sees other families who have more support not doing as well. He feels he also has support and guidance from his math teacher at school. He struggled from a young age with math and now he finally feels confident, not only in math, but in the bigger scheme of life and going to college.

This was a great opening up for the clinician and Xander.

CLOUDS

Purpose

» To identify events or memories that cause sadness or grief.

What you will need

» Photographs of clouds from a recycled magazine

Or

» A window, if it is a cloudy day

Activity

Show the child or adolescent the photographs of clouds. If it is a cloudy day and you have a window, look out at the clouds.

Discuss the idea that people sometimes associate cloudy days with down days or sadness. Ask the child or adolescent to talk about the top two things she feels sad or is grieving about.

Case study: **Child**

Logan is an 11-year-old male who was referred for grief after his mother committed suicide.

The clinician introduces the concept of the Clouds tool to Logan. Logan understands and states he feels like he has had a cloud over him for weeks. When the clinician asks if he can remember when this started, he says when his family first found out that his mother was sick with cancer.

This is a wonderful beginning for Logan and the clinician to work on the issues of sickness and death, ultimately by suicide.

Case study: **Adolescent**

Amelia is a 15-year-old who was referred for depression and underage sex.

The clinician introduces Amelia to the concept of the Clouds tool. She understands the tool and states that she has felt down about herself for a long time. She says that in the beginning of her sophomore year she was very excited about school and was popular. Her boyfriend at the time was a senior and they ended up having sex. Amelia reveals that she felt that after they had sex they would be practically inseparable, and they were, for a while. But then whenever they were together, her boyfriend only wanted to have sex and not do other things. Ultimately, he broke up with her right before prom and ended up taking another girl, with whom Amelia feels he is probably now having sex. She starts to cry at this point. She states she could never tell her parents even though she thinks they may suspect.

This is a good information-gathering session for the clinician and an opportunity for Amelia to talk about her complex issues in a non-threatening environment.

BIRTHDAY BALLOONS 1

Purpose

» To identify special people and their current roles in the child's or adolescent's life.

What you will need

» A drawing of a balloon bouquet
» Markers or colored pencils

Activity

Share with the child or adolescent a copy of the balloon bouquet drawing. Provide him with markers or colored pencils and ask him to fill in all of the people who were present at his last birthday party.

Discuss who was present and what role they play in the individual's life.

Case study: **Child**

Mary is a seven-year-old who was referred for attention deficit hyperactivity disorder and stress.

The clinician explains the Birthday Balloons 1 tool to Mary. She understands and readily writes in the names of people involved in her most recent birthday party. She also has to add some balloons, as there are not enough.

Mary explains that, in her family, birthdays are big celebrations. All of her aunts and uncles and cousins come over. There is food and cake and presents. When asked about the different individuals listed in the balloons, Mary explains that her mom and dad help her, especially with school work, which she reveals she tends to get behind on. She also states that her cousin, who lives on the same street as Mary, comes over after school one day per week to help her with homework.

This was a wonderful opening up and gathering of information for the clinician and Mary.

Case study: **Adolescent**

Wesley is a 16-year-old who was referred for conduct disorder issues.

The clinician explains to Wesley the concept of the Birthday Balloons 1 tool. Wesley understands the concept but does not want to participate in writing. The clinician asks him to just tell her about whom he would place in the balloons.

Wesley would only have two people in the balloons: his mom and his best friend. Wesley is very angry. He reveals there are other people in his family but "they are on his dad's side."

This is a good opening up for the clinician to explore what Wesley means not only by "dad's side," but also how his mom and his best friend are important people in his life.

BALL OF YARN

Purpose

» To collect information about what is confusing or complicated in a child or adolescent's life.

» To aid in bridging memory gaps.

What you will need

» A ball of yarn that looks messy and in some areas is wound tightly

Activity

Show the child or adolescent the ball of yarn. Let her hold it. How would she describe the ball of yarn? All rolled up, messy, lots of it, tight, etc.?

Use the analogy of rolled up, tight or messy to ask the child or adolescent about where she might identify these feelings in her own life.

Case study: **Child**

Riley is a ten-year-old who was referred for issues of peer pressure and anxiety.

The clinician explains the Ball of Yarn tool to Riley. Riley holds the ball of yarn and states that she can totally identify with it. She feels confused and messy and nervous. She reveals that sometimes she feels tightness in her throat when she is nervous.

Her feelings come from her peers expecting her to be able to compete with them in terms of clothes, makeup and boyfriends. Riley feels confused about this. She has moved into the larger middle school, and at her previous primary school, she wore a uniform, so there was no competition for clothes except for shoes. She also states that she can't believe that some of the girls have boyfriends and she does not have one, and she does not want to pretend that she has one like she has in the past.

This is a great opening conversation for the clinician and Riley. She has already brought out many issues that she is struggling with.

Case study: **Adolescent**

Elijah is a 16-year-old who was referred for stress from numerous medical procedures. Elijah has childhood leukemia.

The clinician explains to Elijah the concept of the Ball of Yarn tool. Elijah readily understands the concept. He states that he is many times a ball of yarn. Due to his illness, he has missed so much school he does not even know where to begin. Even though he has not lost a grade level, he believes the teachers just feel sorry for him and let him move ahead. Now he is really struggling.

This is a great opening for Elijah and the clinician. He has revealed the complexity of his issues in a very short period of time.

OUCH!

Purpose

» To gather information regarding physical or emotional hurts or wounds.

What you will need

» Band-Aids

Activity

Show the child or adolescent a box of Band-Aids of all different kinds of sizes and shapes. Discuss the idea that the different Band-Aids are for different kinds of wounds.

Brainstorm different kinds of wounds, physical and emotional. Ask the child or adolescent what kind of wound he is working on now.

Case study: **Child**

Elizabeth is a nine-year-old who was referred for issues of depression and anxiety due to neglect.

The clinician explains the concept of the Ouch! tool. Elizabeth readily understands it. She states that she has had many ouches. One ouch remains with her, and that is something that she is very anxious about: food. Elizabeth reveals that, at her foster care home, the foster care mother padlocks the refrigerator. So after mealtime is over, there is nothing to eat or drink except water and sometimes bananas, if they are available.

This was a good opening up for Elizabeth and the clinician to start to work on a difficult issue.

Case study: **Adolescent**

Jack is a 17-year-old adolescent who was referred for attention deficit hyperactivity disorder and conduct disorder.

The clinician introduces Jack to the concept of the Ouch! tool. He understands the tool and takes out a large gauze bandage. He states that he will need several of these to even begin to cover his hurts. Jack reveals that he has been angry since his teacher called him out in school and made fun of him in front of the entire class. Jack reports that the teacher stated that he will be lucky if he graduates from high school.

This was a good opening up and gathering of information.

HELP!

Purpose

» To gather information in a quick way, especially in imminent situations.

What you will need

» The word "Help!" written on a piece of recycled paper or plastic

Activity

Show the child or adolescent the paper with the word "Help!"

Ask her to brainstorm words and also ideas about areas in which people in her age group might need help. List the ideas on the paper.

Ask the child or adolescent to circle the words with which she would like to have help.

Case study: **Child**

Julianne is an 11-year-old girl who was referred for issues of peer pressure and anxiety.

The clinician introduces Julianne to the concept of the Help! tool. Julianne creates a comprehensive list of what girls her age may be thinking about. She circles nearly everything on the list. She then chooses the top three to start working on.

Julianne was able, on her own, to narrow down her most anxiety-producing issues.

Case study: **Adolescent**

Cole is a 14-year-old who was referred for cyber-addiction, including possible addiction to pornography. He is on probation from school as he was found with pornographic images in his locker.

The clinician explains to Cole the Help! tool. Cole recognizes that he needs help but reveals that he is embarrassed to even create a list.

This is a great opening up and providing of information by Cole for the clinician.

LIFELINES

Purpose

> » To gather information about who or what is supportive in the child's or adolescent's life.

What you will need

> » Paper and pencil or pen

Activity

Introduce the child or adolescent to the concept of lifelines. Have him brainstorm with you about whom or what have been his lifelines, and who or what continue to be his lifelines.

Case study: **Child**

Theo is an eight-year-old who was referred for issues of anxiety due to his parents' divorce. Theo is the only child and is being pulled by both parents.

The clinician introduces Theo to the concept of the Lifelines tool. Theo creates a list of people, including maternal and paternal grandparents, as well as teachers. Theo reveals that both sets of grandparents, as well as both parents, speak ill of each other. This is causing great distress for Theo.

This is a great opening up and providing of information for Theo and the clinician.

Case study: **Adolescent**

Lucia is a 15-year-old new immigrant, who was referred for issues of anxiety and depression.

The clinician introduces Lucia to the concept of the Lifelines tool. Lucia is readily willing to share who her lifelines have been up until her move. Now, Lucia does not know for sure whom her lifelines are. She feels confused about her parents and feels closer to and more able to talk with her teachers, as they are more accepting than her parents.

This was a great opening up and gathering of information for the clinician and Lucia.

NIGHTMARES AND DAYDREAMS

Purpose

» To gather information regarding fears and fantasies.

What you will need

» Only you

Activity

Introduce the child or adolescent to the concepts of nightmares and daydreams. Encourage the child or adolescent to share recent nightmares, or if he or she doesn't have nightmares, ask what would be a nightmare scenario and what would be a daydream or a fantasy scenario.

Case study: **Child**

Oscar is an eight-year-old child who was referred for issues of overeating, diabetes and anxiety.

The clinician shares the concept of the Nightmares and Daydreams tool with Oscar. Oscar readily admits that he has nightmares about his needle sticks. He has this done multiple times per day, even at school. He is frightened by this. His fantasy is that he could be like the other kids and eat whatever he wants. This includes eating hot lunch provided at school.

Oscar revealed many issues in his initial contact with the clinician using the Nightmares and Daydreams tool.

Case study: **Adolescent**

Jocelyn is a 13-year-old who was referred due to physical abuse and neglect.

The clinician shared with Jocelyn the Nightmares and Daydreams tool. Jocelyn states that she has regular nightmares of her mother and her mother's boyfriend beating her. She remembers one particular incident which has become a recurring nightmare. Jocelyn also labels this thought a daydream, as it also occurs during the day.

This information, gathered through the tool, speaks to the depth of the effect that the abuse has caused Jocelyn.

WHY?

Purpose

> » To collect information about how the child or adolescent is feeling about a violent incident or a crisis incident that is hard to understand or come to terms with.

What you will need

> » Only you

Activity

Ask the child or adolescent to talk about her understanding of the trauma or crisis. Remind her that she will not be reliving the event and she will only have to share it one time.

Ultimately, children, adolescents and adults come to the question of why. Why did this happen? Why me? Why her?

Allow the child or adolescent to explore these issues and be able to come to a place of rest and a bit more peace with the incident at this time.

Case study: **Child**

Nicole is a six-year-old girl whose sister was abducted while trying to protect Nicole.

The clinician introduces Nicole to the Why? tool. Nicole starts to cry and shares what happened. Her family does not know where her sister is and she is very scared. She shares multiple questions, such as: Why do people do this? Why did they take her sister? Will they come back for her?

The clinician allows Nicole to share her feelings and then reminds her that she is safe in the present and everyone is taking care of her and watching her and looking for her sister.

This was a very good opening up for a difficult situation.

Case study: **Adolescent**

Deidre is a 16-year-old female who was referred for sexual assault.

The clinician introduces Deidre to the Why? tool. Deidre is readily able to identify with it. She was assaulted by her boyfriend, whom she has known since she was five years old. She doesn't understand how he could do this or why he would do this to her. Deidre is trembling and crying as she talks about the incident. The clinician supports and affirms Deidre.

This was a very good opening up in a delicate and sad crisis event.

BOULDERS

Purpose

» To gather information about and identify obstacles or potential obstacles or difficulties in the child's or adolescent's life.

What you will need

» Photos of boulders from recycled magazines or the Internet

Activity

Allow the child or adolescent to view the photos of boulders. Some may have had the experience of climbing boulders and/or looking at them in nature.

Discuss how boulders may be in the way of streams and how water is diverted around boulders in streams, or how in hiking a path may be blocked by a boulder; yet one can climb over a boulder.

Use this analogy to discuss what "boulders" are in the child's or adolescent's life. What are the issues that he has to circumvent or climb over? What are the obstacles or difficulties?

Case study: **Child**

Brianne is an 11-year-old girl who was referred as she is the new sister of adopted twins who have physical and psychological disabilities.

The clinician explains the Boulders tool. Brianne states that she is having difficulty not feeling negative toward her new siblings. She understands that they are both special needs babies and she herself feels bad for not being more understanding or kind. She also expresses anger toward her parents for not understanding that she, too, needs time. Brianne gives the example that her parents for the first time ever missed one of her conferences at school.

Brianne became engaged and open by using the Boulders tool. She was able to provide the clinician with much information in an initial visit.

Case study: **Adolescent**

Ryker is a 16-year-old adolescent who was referred for issues of anger, physical confrontation with his parents and school truancy.

The clinician introduces Ryker to the Boulders tool. Ryker uses the boulders analogy to state that he has many boulders in his life now and he does not know if he will be able to climb them or get around them. He does know they are permanent and he can't move them. The clinician asks Ryker about the "permanence" of boulders, and Ryker responds that he feels as though he has "screwed up" so much that nothing can undo it. "So why even begin to try?" he asks.

This was a wonderful beginning for Ryker and the clinician. The clinician was able to gather needed information to help Ryker begin to figure out what to do next.

TIMES I NEED

Purpose

» To identify situations in which the child or adolescent self-identifies the need for support.

What you will need

» Dry eraser board

» Markers in two different colors

Activity

Explain to the child or adolescent that there are times in everyone's life where he or she needs some extra help. This help could take the form of physical help, or emotional support/help; for example, listening.

Give an example of when someone might ask for help, such as with homework, or if he or she is being bullied or hurt. Brainstorm together a couple of ideas and write them on a dry eraser board.

Then ask the child or adolescent to identify what she needs. She can just state her needs out loud and you can put them on the dry eraser board with a different-colored marker. That way, she can see quickly which ideas are hers and which are from brainstorming.

Case study: **Child**

Valerie is an eight-year-old who was referred after being removed from her grandmother's home for neglect.

The clinician explains the tool to Valerie. Valerie skips over the part of brainstorming on general needs and goes right to her own. She is much in need of someone to talk with and reveals that she is very frightened and she needs her grandmother and her sisters. (Her older sisters are located in another foster home.)

This was a good opening up for the clinician and Valerie.

Case study: **Adolescent**

Christian is a 16-year-old adolescent who was referred for theft of a vehicle and possession of alcohol.

The clinician introduces Christian to the Times I Need tool. Christian takes off with this tool and skips the step of brainstorming needs. He states that his biggest need is money. He feels constant peer pressure and believes he should be entitled to what he wants when he wants it.

This was a good information gathering for the clinician and Christian.

TIPS FOR CLINICIANS: This tool is a lifelong gift. Reinforce that the individual can use it through his or her entire life.

PUTTING THINGS IN THEIR PLACE

Purpose

» To gather information to determine what needs to happen next.

What you will need

» An old day timer, desk organizer or any type of organizer

Activity

Show the child or adolescent the organizer. Demonstrate the concept that once things are sorted and put in place, it is easier to work with them.

Use this as an analogy to talk about what is going on in the child's or adolescent's life.

Case study: **Child**

Sara is an 11-year-old child who was referred for issues of self-esteem and body image.

The clinician introduces Sara to the Putting Things in Their Place tool. Sara talks about wanting to organize some parts of her life, especially regarding food. She states that she loves sweets and has a hard time controlling her portions. She believes this tendency has led her to use her school lunch money on only sweets. She reveals that other children have begun to make fun of her at school.

This was a good beginning and gathering of information for the clinician and Sara.

Case study: **Adolescent**

Maverick is a 14-year-old adolescent who was referred for anxiety and panic.

The clinician introduces Maverick to the Putting Things in Their Place tool. Maverick states that he needs help. Ever since he started high school, he has been struggling. Maverick reports that he is in advanced placement classes and he also participates in varsity sports.

Maverick states that he is having problems putting all of his activities into order and organizing all of the various demands of school, sports and home.

This was a great beginning for the clinician and Maverick.

TIPS FOR CLINICIANS: This is a lifelong tool, which can be used over and over again. Reinforce this with the individual.

ROCKER

Purpose

> » To identify who or what is calming or soothing in the child's or adolescent's life.

What you will need

> » Any variety of things that could be comforting, such as a soft blanket, socks, teddy bear, rocking chair, etc.

Activity

Discuss with the child or adolescent the idea of what is comforting or soothing for him. For different people it will be different things. Show the child or adolescent some of the things that you have collected. Brainstorm a couple of additional ideas. If you feel comfortable, use self-disclosure to give an example of something that is comforting to you, for example, soft, cozy socks.

Case study: **Child**

Destiny is a ten-year-old child who was referred for eating disorder issues. She is morbidly obese and has been discovered to hoard food in her bedroom.

The clinician introduces Destiny to the Rocker tool. Destiny understands the tool. She states that she likes soft blankets and teddy bears and her dog. She also likes soft socks for comfort. Sometimes when she is hearing her parents yelling, she finds that eating is comforting. She will turn up the TV so that she cannot hear her parents and will grab different snacks. Lately, her mom has been hiding the snacks, but Destiny states she found the snacks and hides them in her room.

This was a good opening up for the clinician and Destiny.

Case study: **Adolescent**

Victoria is a 13-year-old adolescent who was referred for issues of child abuse and neglect.

This is also her third move in foster care.

The clinician introduces Victoria to the Rocker tool. Victoria states there aren't many things she finds comforting. The clinician shows the various items that she has accumulated and asks Victoria if she could brainstorm additional ideas with her.

Victoria states her comfort right now consists of some pictures she carries in her wallet of her brothers. She has not seen her brothers in two years and she is worried about them. She hopes that when her oldest brother turns 18 he "will come for her," if her mom is not better by then.

This tool was very helpful in the gathering of information for the clinician and Victoria.

HIDING

Purpose

> » To gather information about what is scary or what might feel dangerous to face or encounter.

What you will need

> » Only you

Activity

Ask the child or adolescent if she has ever felt like there are times when she would like to hide, or avoid facing certain people, places or events. Determine if any hiding behavior exists now, and what the child or adolescent wants to hide from or avoid facing.

Case study: **Child**

Latisha is a nine-year-old girl who was referred for acting-out behaviors. She has been hitting and kicking other children in the school, and she recently spat on the school bus driver.

The clinician introduces Latisha to the Hiding tool. She states that she is not afraid of anyone or anything and she never hides. In fact, she states that when she feels scared she does the opposite so that people do not know that she is scared: she lashes out.

This was a great gathering of information for Latisha and the clinician.

Case study: **Adolescent**

Stephanie is a 13-year-old who was referred for anxiety and possible social anxiety issues.

The clinician introduces Stephanie to the Hiding tool. Stephanie responds that she is very anxious. She is the youngest person in her freshman year class in high school and also the smallest. She has been called derogatory names and kids have started bullying her because she states she has a good memory and picks up things quickly.

Stephanie reveals that she is hiding in school all of the time. She states that she will pretend to be busy even when she is not because she is afraid and does not want to draw attention to herself. She used to proudly raise her hand in class to answer questions, but now she is not participating as much because she is worried about the social implications from her peers.

This was a good opening up and gathering of information for Stephanie and the clinician.

FEAR

Purpose

» To discover what the child or adolescent is fearful of or worried about.

What you will need

» Worried, fearful and sad emotion faces—these can be drawn on rocks with indelible markers, and used again and again

Activity

Share with the child or adolescent the idea that we all have fears. Some are specific to events or places or even people. Brainstorm different kinds of fears; for example, fear of heights, fear of bears, dogs, bees, etc.

Case study: **Child**

Shawn is an 11-year-old child who was referred for issues of stress and cyber-addiction.

The clinician introduces the Fear tool to Shawn. Shawn responds by helping the clinician to create a list of fears. Shawn states that one of his fears is that he will have his game time taken away, as his parents believe he's addicted to gaming. Shawn tells the clinician that his parents, and sometimes his brother, make fun of his gaming. Shawn has noticed that, as he spends more and more time gaming, he is also becoming increasingly anxious.

This was a good opening up for Shawn and the clinician.

Case study: **Adolescent**

Jacqueline is a 17-year-old adolescent who was referred for depression and cutting behaviors.

The clinician introduces Jacqueline to the Fear tool. Together they create another list, which revolves around burglars, muggers and rapists, and people in general.

Jacqueline reveals that it is difficult for her to trust people, as all through her life people have let her down, from her mom to her present-day teachers.

This was a good initial opening up for Jacqueline and the clinician.

FACES

Purpose

» To gather information about who or what makes the child or adolescent feel soothed or safe when he or she is anxious, fearful or hurt.

What you will need

» Two recycled cans or plates

» Paint

» Paper and pen

Activity

Ask the child or adolescent to paint each can or plate with a face—one happy, and one sad, which could also represent anxiety, fear or hurt.

Create a list of all of the caretakers in the child's or adolescent's life. Ask him, as you name each person on the list, to choose the face that represents that person. Write them all down as he identifies each person. When the exercise is completed, ask which people he would like to talk about. Or talk about how he labeled each individual.

Case study: **Child**

Seth is a six-year-old boy who was referred because his parents have both been incarcerated for physical abuse against his grandmother. Seth is currently living with his aunt.

The clinician introduces Seth to the Faces tool. Seth enjoys painting the cans and using the stickers. Seth is readily able to choose among the cans. He chooses the sad face can for all of his family, including his aunt, with whom he currently lives. He explains that he thinks everyone is sad and hurt and states he has seen his aunt crying. He does not understand why she cries or what has happened to his household.

The clinician works with Seth to think of one person in his life to whom he could give a happy face. Seth states that he is able to give a happy face sometimes to his aunt. The clinician and Seth discuss the idea that although his aunt is crying at times, at other times she is happy and she hugs Seth and his siblings. This allows the clinician to talk with Seth about other family members and the range of emotional states that he observes among them.

This is a great beginning and opening up for Seth and the clinician.

Case study: **Adolescent**

Carlos is a 13-year-old adolescent who was referred for bullying in school and was recently placed on probation for bringing alcohol to school.

The clinician introduces Carlos to the Faces tool. Carlos paints a can and tells the clinician that he does not need a smiley face can because no one is happy with him, not even his best friend. Carlos reveals that his best friend was also placed on school probation because Carlos gave him alcohol, too.

This was a good beginning and opening up for Carlos and the clinician.

STORMS

Purpose

- » To identify who or what is currently difficult or "stormy" in the child's or adolescent's life.

What you will need

- » Old large, clear soda bottle
- » Small pebbles
- » Oil of any kind
- » Sand or dirt, if you wish

Activity

Explain to the child or adolescent that you are going to create a storm in a bottle together. Present her with a large recycled soda bottle.

Ask the child or adolescent to create the storm by adding pebbles, oil, sand or dirt and, finally, water to the bottle. Watch it settle.

Discuss how when it settles, it looks calm. Now, with the cap on the bottle, ask the child or adolescent to shake the bottle.

Discuss how the "storm" looks. Use this as an analogy to talk about storms for self or family.

Case study: **Child**

Harper is a nine-year-old who was referred for grief after her father was killed in a plane crash along with her two brothers. Dad was the pilot.

The clinician introduces Harper to the Storms tool. Harper appears to enjoy assembling the storm in the bottle. She uses the analogy of a storm as what her life has been like since her father and brothers passed away. She feels as if everything is raining down on Harper and her mom, including criticism for her father being a pilot.

This was a wonderful beginning and opening up for Harper and the clinician.

Case study: **Adolescent**

Aaron is a 16-year-old who was referred for distributing pills and a knife at school. The clinician introduces Aaron to the Storms tool. Aaron identifies with it and puts together his bottle. He shakes it and states that he wishes it were carbonated because then it would spray all over everything and that is what's currently happening in his home. He is getting sprayed by a storm. His parents are threatening to have him moved to a military school, his older brother is not talking to him, and he is not sure if the school will be following up with criminal charges.

This was a wonderful opening up and collecting of information for Aaron and the clinician.

RINGING THE BELL

Purpose

» To identify times when the child or adolescent needs to clear some space in his or her head, take a break and maybe ask for help.

What you will need

» A bell of any shape or size

Activity

Ask the child or adolescent to first play with or ring the bell. Adolescents, in particular, might be reluctant to make a noise or bring attention to themselves. Demonstrate that this is OK and is wanted.

Case study: **Child**

Camilia is a ten-year-old who was referred for issues of sexual abuse by her brother, who is 14 years old.

The clinician introduces Camilia to the Ringing the Bell tool. Camilia plays with the bell. She first rings it softly and then very hard and loud. Camilia states that she is angry and that it feels good to ring the bell. Camilia continues to ring the bell and starts to cry. When she stops she is ready to talk.

This was a wonderful opening up and gathering of information on where Camilia is during this difficult time.

Case study: **Adolescent**

Devin is a 15-year-old who was referred for anger and vandalism issues.

The clinician introduces Devin to the Ringing the Bell tool. Devin rings the bell immediately and states that he knows why he is here (in the office), and he says he thinks that the clinician already has a preconceived notion of Devin being a bad kid or, as Devin states, a "delinquent."

This was a wonderful initial opening up and gathering of information for Devin and the clinician.

A TIME WHEN MY HEART WAS OPEN

Purpose

» To allow the child or adolescent to remember a time when he or she felt quiet internally, safe and at peace; a time when his or her heart felt open.

What you will need

» Only you

Activity

Discuss with the child or adolescent the idea of a memory or a moment in time when he felt complete peace. Suggestions could be: alone in his room, with a companion animal, in a special place, such as near a body of water, in nature, or even during a special family time.

Ask the child or adolescent to close his eyes (if he doesn't feel comfortable closing his eyes, that's OK) and think about a moment in time, a memory, in as much detail as he can, or a time when he felt at peace and his heart felt open. Use all senses, such as remembering the temperature, the smell, the color, etc.

Allow a minute or two for the child or adolescent to remember and then ask how he feels. Remind him that he can go back there and feel that safety and open heart at any time, simply by remembering.

Case study: **Child**

Anita is a ten-year-old who was referred for anxiety, panic attacks and night terrors. Anita found her mother and her mother's boyfriend unconscious. The only other adult in the household had fled.

The clinician introduces Anita to the A Time When My Heart Was Open tool. Anita is able to remember a lovely time in the park when she was swinging with her friends. She remembers having a swinging race to see who could swing the highest. Anita states she felt free and happy and was full of energy at the time.

This tool was effective in helping Anita remember positive times and ways of coping through the use of memories.

Case study: **Adolescent**

Cliff is a 12-year-old who was referred for anxiety with panic and depression. Cliff witnessed his younger sibling being molested, and he and his sibling, as well as the family's pet cat, were threatened with harm if he told.

The clinician introduces Cliff to the A Time When My Heart Was Open tool. Cliff remembers many times when his heart felt open before the traumatic event; however, there was one time he thinks of often. He and his family were on a vacation and he was able to see the ocean. He remembers hearing the waves and walking in the water. As Cliff talks about his memory, the clinician can see his face relax and his breathing deepen.

This was a great tool for helping Cliff to cope.

FUN

Purpose

» To remember times when the child or adolescent was not in trauma or crisis.

» To normalize and help cope.

What you will need

» Only you

Activity

Have the child or adolescent recount a fun or joyous time in her life. Have her talk about emotional and physical feelings.

Case study: **Child**

Lexi is a ten-year-old who was referred after she experienced paralysis in her left leg due to abuse by her biological father.

The clinician explained to Lexi the Fun tool. Lexi remembered a time recently where she had a fun time eating pizza and playing games with her grandmother and brother. Lexi talked about having feelings of relief and relaxation in her body and mind.

This was a wonderful opening up and gathering of information for the clinician and Lexi.

Case study: **Adolescent**

Linda is a 16-year-old who was referred for eating disorder issues which started at the age of 11.

The clinician introduced Linda to the Fun tool. Linda started to cry and stated that she has many memories from when she was ten and younger of having fun but that they all surround eating.

This was a wonderful beginning for Linda and the clinician.

Part 3

POSITIVE THINKING

MASK OF ME × 3

Purpose

» To have the child or adolescent express an image of self in the past, present and future.

What you will need

» Three masks

» Paint, glitter, feathers—whatever you have in art supplies

Activity

Help the child or adolescent make a mask or a group of masks representing different times or periods in his life. For example, we can create Past, Present and Future Masks. This project can be completed over a series of appointments.

Provide the child or adolescent with plastic masks that represent either a full or partial face. Some children prefer a full mask, whereas others prefer a mask that shows their mouth so that they can demonstrate emotions using their mouths, such as smiles, frowns, terror, etc., while still wearing the mask. For some, this mask is an insulator and allows them to show feelings that may be scary or too difficult to show if they did not have the aid of the mask.

Many children and adolescents like to begin this project with the Past Mask. The Past Mask, for most individuals, represents what brought them in for help. This is a difficult mask to make. Many children and adolescents will be hesitant to begin. Remind them that they are not reliving their experience; rather, they are expressing what it felt like.

At this time, it is appropriate to show the child or adolescent other masks that have been completed by other individuals of a similar age. Note the intensity of the masks and the different colors and textures utilized. Explain that the mask that he is about to make may not be pretty or attractive but, instead, may be dark or even scary looking.

If you do not have other masks available, it's OK to talk about examples of masks you have witnessed. I have seen masks completely painted black, or black, blue and red masks. I even saw a mask that was painted completely white with a gold smudge on the forehead that represented the individual's brain. For that person, even though what he had gone through was unbelievable and he still felt very much as if he were walking through a fog at the time, he also remembered having some good things happen during the bad times. This was quite remarkable, as it was the only such mask I have seen that mentioned the good during the past.

You are talking about and showing the different ways that individuals may feel about the past and how the masks represent their feelings. It is very important that you accept whatever comes up for the child or adolescent at this time. I have had children who used sandpaper on their masks and some who have even made cut marks. The goal here for the adult is to be constant, steady and supportive. The individual with whom we are working hasn't had any of these during that time in the past. Any sense of judgment may cause alienation from the project or even from the process as a whole. Take your time, and be gentle and encouraging.

Sometimes I put on soft background music to allow us to be present and comforted while we work on the Past Mask. I will also work on a mask myself next to the child. He may notice mine along the way or simply be more comfortable that I am not observing him too closely. This is also a good time to give gentle praise along the way, such as, "This is a hard project, but I am glad you are getting started." Or: "You have chosen some dark colors. I am looking forward to learning what they mean for you."

Sometimes this takes more than one session. Usually, these projects should be done in the office setting and not taken home.

Give the child or adolescent a choice to talk about each mask as it is completed or to wait until all of the masks are completed. As the child or adolescent shares his feelings about her Past Mask, remember to start out with praise. This may very well be the first time that he has brought his trauma out in a nonverbal way. It may be a relief but also discomforting. Allow the child or adolescent to slowly explain the meaning of the colors, the brush strokes, the cuts or anything which the child places on the mask. Empathize how scary, difficult, sad, etc. it must have been. Make sure to remind the child that this was from the past. He is safe now.

At this time, the child or adolescent may be exhausted, frustrated, angry or tearful. Allow the feelings and help them slowly dissipate by bringing the client back into the present with a discussion of what the next meeting will look like. Remind the individual that he can discuss the Past Mask at any time and that you will keep it in a safe place for him and he can have it or leave it here when the project is completed. The next time you meet, it will be to do the Present Mask. The Present Mask will illustrate where the individual is now. It will show how he is coping or not coping. It may show anguish, fear or frustration, or feelings such as hope or wanting to forget.

In the next session, open up by asking if the individual would like to talk more about the Past Mask; if not, move on to the Present Mask. Again, show examples of completed masks from children of the same age range. If there are not any available, sit down with the individual and work side by side on your own mask. Show the child or adolescent the variety of materials that can be used on the mask. Encourage the child as he works on his mask. If it feels comfortable, you can begin a dialog about how it feels in the present. Otherwise, again play soft, comforting music in the background.

Again, allow the child or adolescent enough time to complete this mask. It may take two meetings. When the child has completed the project, or a few minutes before the session is over, give him an opportunity to talk about how he feels about the mask. He may or may not want to talk about it, and that is OK. He may want to think about it until the next meeting. Remind the child or adolescent about what will take place next time: discussion if he wants or needs it, and then beginning work on the Future Mask.

In the next session, open up by asking the individual if he would like to talk more about the Present Mask; if not, move on to the Future Mask.

Encourage the child or adolescent to be free-flowing and to really look closely at the art supplies available. It is during this part of the project that we see hope, fun and even some silliness or laughter. It has not been uncommon in my practice to have feathers flying or glitter raining down! Children or adolescents should be supported in this, their Future Mask. What colors, textures, etc. do they want to use? I have seen flowers, both plastic and painted on, along with felt and other materials used. Their imagination is the limit! Some children or adolescents like to talk at this time; some may joke or giggle internally.

If you are making a mask next to them, you may find yourself doing the same! Let it flow—be natural and supportive. The child or adolescent you are working with is about to create hope!

Allow the child or adolescent two sessions, if needed, to complete this mask. During the final meeting for this project, the child or adolescent will have the opportunity to share how he feels about the future. For many, working with the scented markers, flowers, glitter, stamps, etc. has been fun and powerful. For children and adolescents who have been through trauma, we—and they—sometimes forget the power of fun. Fun allows for peace in the moment and a general sense of well-being, as well as hope for the future! This future hope is, of course, a goal when working with our traumatized youth.

The discussion begins. We may start with the Future Mask and talk about what the colors and textures symbolize for that individual. Then we review all the masks. We draw attention to the progression in the masks—the difference in emotional states. Discuss awareness of change and how things have already changed from the past to the present. Look at the Future Mask and discuss it. Ask questions such as: "What is the first little step that we can take to move toward the feelings and emotions in the Future Mask?"; and "What is something that can be done today or this week that would help us to get closer to the Future Mask?"; and "What is a big goal, a long-term goal, that would help you to achieve the Future Mask?"

Take time to brainstorm ideas. If the child or adolescent gets stuck and is not sure what to say, a good question could be: "What is one thing you could do for yourself today or this week that would make you feel good about yourself or happy? Perhaps meeting with a friend, playing a game, going for a walk, playing with a dog or cat, calling a relative, or eating an ice cream cone?"

Finally, review all three masks together. Review gently what the individual felt in the Past Mask. Acknowledge those feelings and also demonstrate through review of the Present Mask where the individual is now. Discuss the changes between the two masks. New feelings and emotions may come up at this time. Reassure the child or adolescent that this is OK. It is normal to notice the changes and to have an emotional response. You might state, "That was very difficult then, and this is now. It is different."

Continue to move forward to the comparison with the Future Mask with all of its hope. Reinforce with children or adolescents the hard work they did to complete this project. Congratulate them. They may choose to take home the masks or leave one or more with you for other children or adolescents to see as a reminder that they are not alone.

Case study: **Child**

Emily is a nine-year-old girl who was referred for issues of anger, acting out and an incident of exposing her genitals to a boy at school. The clinician explains the technique to Emily and shows her examples of masks that other children have created. Emily comments on the masks, stating that one of them looks very sad and another looks angry. She is excited to get started on her mask. For her Past Mask, she combines all of the colors available, which turn into a blackish-blue color. As Emily is working on her mask, she becomes quite animated and places her paintbrush in the container quite hard. She states she feels angry and she feels down. She feels like she is in trouble all of the time and she begins to cry.

The clinician reassures Emily that she is not in trouble and reinforces the good work that she is doing. Again, the clinician refers to the masks that other children have made and talks about how others have expressed negative feelings. The clinician reminds Emily that having negative feelings does not make us bad and she is definitely not in trouble. In fact, she is well on her way to completing the project. Emily can now relax and reflect on her work. She can return to her mask in the following session.

Emily returns to her session and the clinician compliments her on her work. Emily states that in the past she felt like, no matter what she did, she was always in trouble with her family, school and friends.

After discussing this, Emily asks to get started on her second mask, the Present Mask. This is completed quickly and is painted entirely brown. She states that bad things have happened and it is difficult to talk about them. The clinician and the child take time with this mask to find out what it means and what "bad" things have happened that she *does* feel she can talk about. (The clinician will revisit this issue when they review all three masks, and Emily feels more safe and confident.)

Emily's final mask is pink with some feathers and rhinestones on it. She states her favorite color is pink and that she likes to see and wear this color. She also likes sparkly things and talks about some things which she is looking forward to doing with her friends over her school break.

Emily and the clinician review all three masks. Emily can see how her emotions have changed over time. She is also able to identify in her final mask times when she is not so distressed and is looking forward to her future with hope.

Emily was able to overcome her reluctance to engage with the clinician by utilizing masks that she could literally hide behind in the beginning, if she chose. Masks are also an interesting object for children of this age.

Case study: **Adolescent**

Kaley is a 15-year-old girl, referred for issues of depression, anxiety and possible sexual abuse. She has been cutting herself on and off for the past two years. The clinician explains the technique to Kaley, and shows completed masks that others have made. She explains that some teens want her to keep the masks to show others. They look at each mask together and discuss the meanings. Kaley is ready to start her own mask. As she works on her mask and starts to paint it different colors, she begins to talk about how she feels and what the colors mean.

Kaley was able to overcome her reluctance to engage with the clinician by utilizing the vehicle of the masks. She was able to portray how she felt in a safe way.

TIPS FOR CLINICIANS: This tool can elicit strong memories and sometimes grief. The final section of the activity, the Future Mask, is critical in creating hope. Take extra time here if you need to and help the child or adolescent to envision on the mask a better future and what it would feel like.

TREASURE BOX

Purpose

» To discover what the child or adolescent feels are treasures or very special events, such as people or things in his or her life.

» To reinforce positive aspects already in the life of the child or adolescent.

» To reinforce the child's or adolescent's positive memories.

What you will need

» Shoe box or recycled box of any type with a lid or cover

» Paint, fabric, glue, other art supplies

» Faux gold coins, jewels

Activity

Help the child or adolescent create a treasure box out of a shoe box or any box with a lid. The box should feel special for the individual making it. The clinician may want to talk about what an individual adolescent or child imagines a treasure chest to look like. Some individuals may think of an old trunk; others may have the idea of a small jewel box or a display container for special items. The box should look attractive to that individual, a place where she would put special things to keep and cherish. The individual can paint the box both inside and out. Some children and adolescents have, in addition to painting the box, lined it with fabric, feathers or rhinestones. Allow adequate time to decorate the box. The clinician may play soft music and engage in making his or her own treasure box while the child or adolescent is working on hers.

Place one rhinestone or one fake gold coin in the treasure box to represent something precious. Talk about what precious means. Ask the child or adolescent to think about what she has in her life that she would consider precious or a treasure.

Ask the child or adolescent to write down what she has identified as precious or treasures on slips of paper that the clinician provides, and place the slips of paper into the treasure box.

Take time to review what is in the treasure chest. Ask her to share what is on the slips of paper and discuss their meaning. Reinforce with the individual the many positives that she identified. Remind her that she has many valuable or precious people, memories, events, animals, etc. in her life!

Allow the child or adolescent to take the treasure box home as a memory and reinforcement of positives in her life. She can look into the memory box any time she needs encouragement or wants to remember the positives. As time goes by, she can also add more to her treasure box.

Case study: **Child**

Carrie is a ten-year-old girl referred for panic attacks. She was photographed while in different stages of undress by her male cousin, who is 14 years old.

The clinician presents Carrie with the treasure box and explains the technique. Initially, it is difficult for Carrie to get started. She begins by looking through the "jewels" and plastic rhinestones and shiny things. She likes the colors and the shine and begins to glue and cover her entire box inside and out with the gems.

Her slips of paper or treasures demonstrate that she has many good friends and family members, all of whom are precious to her. On the inside of the box, she places a plastic dog and glues the dog in. She states that if her dog had been with her at the time of the incident she would have been safe. This statement allows the clinician an entrance into exploring the event with Carrie.

Carrie was able to overcome her reluctance to engage with the clinician by being stimulated and interested in the sparkly plastic jewels. She wanted to use them, to handle them and to keep them as part of the take-home project. This ultimately led to a much deeper conversation.

Case study: **Adolescent**

A 16-year-old female, Samantha, was referred for issues of depression and cutting. Her biological mom is an alcoholic in recovery. Dad works long hours and is unavailable. The clinician explains the technique to Samantha and hands her a small wooden box. The clinician makes available a wide range of art supplies. Samantha chooses to decorate her box in paint and glitter. She even puts glitter on the inside of the box. The clinician asks Samantha about the glitter and its meaning. Samantha starts to smile and states she has many good memories and will need more than one jewel so that she can talk about the good. The clinician and Samantha recognize there is a mixture of good and bad, metaphorically, in the box.

Samantha was able to overcome her reluctance to engage with the clinician by immediately being attracted to the glitter and paint. It seemed to stir many feelings for her. These were materials that were familiar and with which she was comfortable. Even though she had not used them in some time, she enjoyed them. This art vehicle allowed Samantha to move out of her current thoughts and into a creative mode, in which she was readily able to engage. Samantha enjoyed the tool and created many slips of paper to place in her treasure box.

TIPS FOR CLINICIANS: This is a particularly useful tool for adolescents. When using with younger children, I sometimes ask the child to draw pictures on the sheets of paper instead of words.

GREEN FLASH

Purpose

» To identify thoughts and feelings which are present but may not be obvious to the clinician or to others.

What you will need

» Photos from the Internet or access to a computer or tablet

Activity

Introduce the child or adolescent to the phenomenon of the "green flash." The clinician may start by stating that they will begin their discussion by talking about a natural phenomenon that occurs daily, but which the individual has probably never noticed or knew existed. The clinician may self-disclose if she or he had known about it before learning about this tool or had ever seen it.

Share with the child or adolescent this definition of the green flash:

Green flashes and green rays are optical phenomena that occur shortly after sunset or before sunrise, when a green spot is visible, usually for no more than a second or two, above the sun, or it may resemble a green ray shooting up from the sunset point.

Ask the child or adolescent if he has ever heard of the green flash or seen it. Present a photograph, which can be obtained from the Internet. Discuss how interesting it is that most people have never seen or known of the green flash even though it exists every day. Discuss the idea that things exist that some people, such as scientists, are aware of, but others may not know about unless they are told.

Ask the child or adolescent if he has any "green flashes." Some individuals may respond with situations that are happening on a daily basis in their homes or schools. Others may have thoughts or memories that come up daily and no one else knows about them.

Case study: **Child**

Eleven-year-old Sharman was referred to the office after being the first person to find his mother had committed suicide in a violent manner.

The clinician and Sharman talk about the Green Flash tool. Sharman is impressed with the concept and states it is "cool." Sharman reveals that he might have actually seen the green flash. He goes on to talk about how he is quite observant and he thinks he may have recognized the extent to which his mom was sad. He expresses guilt for not behaving better and maybe contributing to his mother's sadness. He also has several sudden images of the week prior to his mom's death when Mom was fine and actually laughing and happy. These statements allow the clinician to continue to explore feelings of guilt, as well as help the child to understand he is not part of the reason Mom committed suicide.

Sharman was able to overcome his reluctance to engage with the clinician by engaging first in the concept of the green flash and talking about how "cool" it was. This allowed him to be OK with something different and out of the ordinary, something almost unbelievable. It allowed him to talk about his mother's suicide.

Case study: **Adolescent**

Fourteen-year-old Nevins was physically and sexually abused by his biological mom's boyfriend. Nevins has been acting out in school and threatening other children. The clinician explains to Nevins the phenomenon of the green flash. She shows him a photograph as well as a slow-motion exposure from the Internet. Nevins is thrilled—he can't believe it. The clinician and Nevins talk about how things happen around us every day and we may not be aware of them.

During the discussion, Nevins starts to cry. He states that he feels like screaming or punching something. He expresses that he is angry with his mother, grandmother and teacher for not knowing that he was being abused.

Nevins was able to overcome his reluctance to engage with the clinician because of his interest in the scientific phenomenon. It was new and exciting and he could immediately relate to it.

CLEAN THE MIRROR

Purpose

» To gather information and help the child or adolescent remove or change issues that are causing concern or emotional pain.

What you will need

» A hand mirror

Activity

The clinician presents a hand mirror to the child or adolescent, and explains that when we have a clean mirror, we can accurately see what is reflected. The clinician can discuss with the child or adolescent things that distort mirrors, such as steam, smudges from fingers, dust, etc. When there is something in the way, we cannot see the bigger picture clearly.

The clinician uses this analogy to discuss what might be in the way or cause a distortion in a child's life.

Case study: **Child**

Sitmala is a ten-year-old girl who was referred for eating disorder issues, which started after she was bullied by the other girls at school. She is overweight and knows this. Prior to the bullying, she had been working on a diet and exercise program prescribed by her doctor. Since the bullying began, Sitmala was caught binging and vomiting at home. She has also been caught at school with laxatives, which she took from her home medicine cabinet. Her parents are worried that she may be self-harming as well.

The clinician meets with Sitmala and explains the tool. Sitmala states that she can't look in the mirror because all she sees is fat. She states she is ugly and fat and now no one likes her at school. She reveals that at times she feels like running away.

Sitmala and the clinician discuss how things, including ideas about ourselves, might get distorted, just as if we are looking at a distorted mirror at a carnival. The clinician gently asks Sitmala if she will look into the mirror briefly and find just one feature or aspect about herself that she likes.

She finds three: her hair, her eyes and her skin.

This is a good place for the clinician and the child to start to deconstruct the perceptions of being ugly and begin to work on the weight and eating disorder issue.

Case study: **Adolescent**

Anton is a 17-year-old adolescent who was referred for issues of aggression with his parents and defiance. In addition, he was recently accused by a peer of molestation.

Anton presents with bravado. He states that he knows what this is about, and when the clinician describes the Clean the Mirror tool, Anton says he doesn't have to look into it because he has done nothing wrong and further states that everyone likes him. When asked about the recent accusation, he states that the girl was jealous of him and wanted to get back because he has a new girlfriend.

The clinician and Anton talk about the idea that maybe the mirror isn't big enough. Maybe he is not seeing everything—maybe he is only seeing himself. What does he think his parents feel about this accusation? Are they worried, angry, neutral? Anton begins to open up and talk about the idea that he actually is worried and needs to figure out what to do next as the police are involved and his parents want him to live with his uncle.

This is a great step for Anton's progress. He opened up and the clinician was able to gather information to start to plan for helping Anton.

TIPS FOR CLINICIANS: Watch for self-criticism and self-blame and direct the child or adolescent toward information gathering.

GARDEN OF GRIEF

Purpose

» To help open up and release sad or grieving emotions.

What you will need

» Old magazines with garden photos

Activity

Show the child or adolescent photos of beautiful gardens or park scenes. Talk about memory gardens/parks or tribute gardens/parks. Some of these could include our national gardens or smaller gardens, or even roadside garden tributes.

Ask the individual if she has ever seen any of these types of gardens. Discuss what they mean. Many of the national gardens have descriptive placards, which can be seen on the Internet. Ask her to talk about her interpretation of what the placards describe. Some contain statues commemorating certain individuals. Ask the individual how she feels about these kinds of tributes.

Case study: **Child**

Corrinne is a nine-year-old girl who was referred for therapy, as her adoptive grandfather recently passed away. Corrinne is adopted and has reactive detachment disorder. She has been expressing sadness and even talking about wanting to die herself.

When the clinician meets with Corrinne and discusses the use of the Garden of Grief tool, Corrinne immediately becomes tearful. She states that she misses her grandfather so much and does not understand why God took him. She expresses feelings of loneliness even though she has a biological sister and two other adopted siblings in the family.

She states that her siblings are not as sad as she is. Her mom gave her a photograph of her grandpa to keep on her dresser. She states that this has helped.

The clinician asks if it would be helpful to create a garden on paper for her grandfather. As Corrinne creates the garden, she talks about her grandfather and about the idea that at times she would like to die so that she could be with him.

Obviously, this was a powerful statement to which the clinician was able to respond.

Case study: **Adolescent**

Jada is a 16-year-old female who was referred after her boyfriend and his brother were killed in a car crash.

The clinician explains the Garden of Grief tool. Jada expresses sadness, anger and fear. She states that where her boyfriend and his brother passed away there is a huge roadside commemoration. "So much has been placed there that the police have asked people to stop adding things as it is becoming distracting for drivers."

Jada expresses helplessness. She does not know what to do or how to even begin to believe what happened. She reveals that she still waits for her boyfriend to call her.

This is a wonderful beginning to helping Jada.

GARDEN OF HOPE

Purpose

» To gather information about what brings hope or what one is hopeful for.

What you will need

» Old magazines with garden photos

Activity

Show the client photos of all different types of gardens: water gardens, Japanese gardens, English gardens, serenity gardens, vegetable gardens, etc.

Discuss how the child or adolescent feels when exposed to each garden. Identify particular elements that he finds hopeful or peaceful, such as statues or ornaments, particular flowers or shrubs, or perhaps the curve of a garden path.

Case study: **Child**

Max is a five-year-old boy who was referred for issues of crying and screaming when he is separated from his mom, such as when attending school or any time she leaves the room. He has also recently started to wet the bed. Max recently moved with his mom and dad from Japan, where he had lived with his parents, paternal grandmother, uncle and aunt.

The clinician introduces Max to the Garden of Hope tool. She shows him various garden photos. When he sees the Japanese garden scene he tells her this is what his grandmother's garden looks like. He then starts to express how he misses his grandmother. The clinician and Max talk about how everything is new for him: new people, new schools, even new gardens, and how that is really a hard transition.

The clinician was able to establish rapport and gather information about the level of difficulty Max was experiencing as he and his family established themselves in a new country.

Case study: **Adolescent**

Fatima is a 15-year-old girl who was referred for issues of depression, anxiety and cutting. Her family recently emigrated from the Middle East.

The clinician introduces Fatima to the tool. Fatima enjoys looking at the garden photos. She tells the clinician that she used to wish that someday she would be able to travel and visit some of the beautiful gardens around the world. She has seen many already in various travels with her parents.

She reveals that she no longer believes she will be able to do that. She states that she has been struggling with her grades in school and that her parents are pressuring her to earn all A grades. Fatima feels as though she has been doing the best that she can. She has a tutor three times per week, plus she sees her instructors regularly for extra help. She reveals that her parents have told her that if she does not do well in school and receive high grades, she will fail in life. She feels immense pressure to outshine everyone.

Fatima has revealed the complexity of what she is dealing with. This is a good beginning for her.

TIPS FOR CLINICIANS: This tool can be referred to throughout the entire therapeutic relationship. It is a powerful reminder of hope and positive feelings.

WISH UPON A STAR 2

Purpose

- » To increase self-esteem.
- » To increase self-awareness.
- » To ascertain wants, needs, goals.

What you will need

- » Recycled cardboard
- » Foil
- » Glitter, glue, construction paper, paint, ribbon, etc.

Activity

Have the child/adolescent make a star for herself and ask her, "What would your wish be?" Have her make a star for someone else and name who it would be for. Ask her, "What would you wish for them? What would their wish be? Would they make a wish for you? If so, what would it be?"

Case study: **Child**

Erin is eight. She was referred for issues of scratching herself and hitting herself in the head, arms and chest.

The clinician introduces Erin to the Wish Upon a Star 2 tool. Erin creates a large star out of cardboard. She draws her star and colors it light blue. She colors the surrounding area in black to represent the night sky.

Erin reveals that she has many wishes. She wishes that she had a sibling. She also wishes that her grandparents lived closer. Most of all, she wishes her parents would stop fighting. Her parents yell and "push" each other in front of her. When this happens, Erin feels like screaming, but instead she will scratch herself with her own nails.

Sometimes, if she hears them fighting while she is in her room, she will hit herself, "just to make all the noise stop."

By talking about wishes, the clinician is able to get Erin to describe her situation.

Case study: **Adolescent**

Serena is a 16-year-old female who was referred for issues of depression and suicidal ideation.

When the clinician introduces Serena to the Wish Upon a Star 2 tool, Serena states that she just wishes everything would go away. She is sick of her parents, her school and even her friends. She has been having these feelings since her boyfriend broke up with her. She wishes her history would disappear and that she could start fresh in a new school with new friends.

This was a good opening up and gathering of information for Serena and the clinician.

MAKE YOURSELF A STAR

Purpose

» To help the child/adolescent to identify what is already great about himself or herself.

» To increase self-esteem and self-confidence.

What you will need

» Recycled cardboard

» Glue, glitter, miscellaneous art supplies

Activity

Have the child make a star that reflects who she is. For example, her star could be made pink with pink glitter and silver foil, or whatever she decides. Reflect on stars: how stars shine, how stars glitter at night, how stars are bright, etc.

Ask, "What makes you a star? In what way in your own life are you already a star? How could you shine brighter? How do you feel on the inside? Glittery?"

Explore further: "How could you feel glittery on the inside and out? What would you need to feel that way? Could anyone help you? If so, who and how?"

Case study: **Child**

Paisley is an 11-year-old who has been referred for feelings of anxiety and panic, accompanied by weight loss.

The clinician explains the Make Yourself a Star tool, and Paisley creates a large, pink glittery star. She finds and discusses many things that make her shine: her friends, her parents—especially her mom—and her sisters. She states that she usually glows inside but lately she has butterflies. Paisley has been experiencing bullying at school to the point where the bully has threatened physical harm.

This was a great opening up and gathering of information for Paisley and the clinician.

Case study: **Adolescent**

Hudson is a 13-year-old boy who was referred for isolation and cyber-addiction. Hudson creates a large blue star. He finds many things, especially things about himself, that make him feel good. He is good at math, computers and even robotics. He also loves to play competitive games on the Internet, but he reveals that his parents think he spends too much time on that. He believes the more time he spends, the better he will become at all of his skills.

This is a great opening up for Hudson and the clinician.

LUCK

Purpose

» To identify times in the child's or adolescent's life when he or she felt good and that something positive happened that was unexpected, either through a person or an event.

What you will need

» Recycled cardboard or a green soda bottle

» Markers

Activity

Have ready a four-leaf clover made out of cardboard or a green soda bottle. Have a dark marker available to write on the four-leaf clover. Explain to the individual the idea behind the lucky clover and what it means.

Could she describe times in her life when she felt lucky or something good happened, which maybe she did not expect? This could happen in a place, with a person or during an event or anything else she can think of. Ask her to write on the four-leaf clover things she feels good about or lucky to have.

Case study: **Child**

Five-year-old Katie was referred for transition from an orphanage in Russia to her new home in the United Kingdom. She has issues of night terrors and anxiety, possibly reactive detachment disorder and post-traumatic stress disorder.

The clinician asks Katie if she knows about the concept of the four-leaf clover. Katie states that she does not, so the clinician explains the meaning and also shows her a real four-leaf clover in a paperweight.

Katie takes her four-leaf clover made out of construction paper and writes two words: "Mom" and "Dad."

This gave the clinician and the child an opening, which they needed to move forward.

Case study: **Adolescent**

Tibor is a 16-year-old adolescent who was referred for issues of vandalizing neighbors' properties and his own parents' car.

Tibor is introduced to the Luck tool. He states that he has a lot of luck. One of his biggest kinds of luck is that he is a minor and he can't be prosecuted. Tibor takes the four-leaf clover and writes very quickly. He writes that he is lucky to be smart and from a wealthy family. He writes that his parents and grandparents love him and that he has many friends.

It doesn't seem to have much of an impact on Tibor that he is no longer able to play sports in high school due to his behaviors and involvement in the legal system.

This revelation of how Tibor truly feels allowed an opening with the clinician to help Tibor better understand the larger scope of his behaviors.

WHAT HAPPINESS LOOKS LIKE

Purpose

- » To identify what happiness means to the child or adolescent.
- » To identify current sources of happiness in his or her life.

What you will need

- » Paint
- » Crayons
- » Markers
- » Recycled cardboard or plastic

Activity

Have the child or adolescent paint or draw what happiness looks like to him.

Case study: **Child**

Joy is a nine-year-old who was referred for issues of anger and acting out in school and at home.

The clinician introduces Joy to the What Happiness Looks Like tool. Joy states that she loves to paint and she frequently paints at home. Joy chooses a large piece of recycled cardboard and uses yellow, orange and pink. She states she is painting the sun and that happiness is being with her family on a sunny day. Joy adds that she enjoys her time with her family, but that she is not able to spend much time with them, as her older siblings drive, work and have other friends with whom she is not included.

This was a good opening up and gathering of information for Joy and the clinician.

Case study: **Adolescent**

Declan is a 15-year-old who was referred for issues of anger, property damage and physical fighting at school.

The clinician introduces Declan to the What Happiness Looks Like tool. Declan uses markers and a pen to draw a house in a very specific way. Declan states that this was his family's old house that he lived in when his father was alive. Declan reveals that his father died when he was 11. He further reveals that his father was involved in a gang and that now he himself is involved in a gang and is afraid to try to get out of the gang.

This was a good opening up and gathering of information for Declan and the clinician.

TIPS FOR CLINICIANS: This tool can be used throughout the therapeutic process. It is a strong reminder and reinforcement of the positive.

MAGIC WAND

Purpose

» To identify areas of desired change.

» To reinforce and acknowledge the child's or adolescent's feelings, wants and needs.

What you will need

» Only you, or if you choose, a magic wand made out of straws or Popsicle sticks, decorated with ribbons or feathers

Activity

Ask the child or adolescent: If she had a magic wand and she could wave it over her life and present circumstances, what would she change or want to be different?

The individual can talk about safe and funny things at first, and then move into discussing what other things she might change.

Case study: **Child**

Eleanor is a seven-year-old who was referred after both of her parents were incarcerated for drug manufacturing and distribution.

The clinician introduces Eleanor to the Magic Wand tool. Eleanor plays with the wand, which the clinician had made out of Popsicle sticks, ribbon and paint. Eleanor talks about changing everything and getting her parents back to her home but only after they got help. The clinician asks Eleanor what she means by "got help," and she answers that her grandmother, with whom she now lives, told her that her parents have problems and were doing bad things that they should never have done with Eleanor and her siblings in the house.

This was a good opening up and collecting of information for Eleanor and the clinician.

Case study: **Adolescent**

Gideon is a 16-year-old who was referred on allegations of raping another student during a party where there was underage drinking.

The clinician introduces Gideon to the Magic Wand tool. Gideon immediately states that he wishes he could undo most of the past year. Ultimately, he reveals that he was under the influence of alcohol, as well as drugs, and he is not sure if the allegations of rape are true or not. He reveals he feels miserable and even suicidal.

This was a crucial opening up and gathering of information for Gideon and the clinician.

FEATHERS—TICKLE

Purpose

- » To help children or adolescents to identify things which make them laugh.
- » To remember and reinforce funny times and good memories.

What you will need

- » Feathers in a bowl

Activity

Give the child or adolescent a plastic bowl filled with feathers and let him feel the feathers.

Talk about how feathers can tickle and make us laugh.

Ask him to remember funny times and identify who he was with, and what happened.

Case study: **Child**

Juliette is a six-year-old who was referred for sadness and grief after her father passed away from a long-term illness.

Juliette is introduced to the Feathers—Tickle tool. Juliette enjoys playing with the bowl of feathers. As the discussion progresses, she remembers many happy, funny times with her dad and that she also has had some recent fun times with her brother, her uncle and her grandfather.

This was a good opening up and gathering of information for Juliette and the clinician.

Case study: **Adolescent**

Sawyer is a 16-year-old who was referred after his twin brother was paralyzed after a car accident that occurred when Sawyer was driving.

Sawyer is introduced to the Feathers—Tickle tool. Sawyer reveals that he does everything he can to help his twin have fun and be happy, but that he, himself, is really struggling. He has many good memories of the two of them having adventures like camping, rock climbing, swimming and bicycling. He did have a recent fun time with his twin when his family created a bonfire and they all talked about good old memories and planning for the future, including future family trips and how to accommodate his brother.

This was a wonderful opening up and gathering of information for the clinician and Sawyer.

LOTUS

Purpose

» To discover the strengths and supports, as well as what creates resiliency, in a child's or adolescent's life.

What you will need

» Photos of a lotus plant from a recycled garden magazine or other magazine, or printed off the Internet

Activity

Read a short history of the lotus, including how resilient it is. The oldest viable seed in history is from a lotus that is 1300 years old. In addition, the lotus grows in conditions that most other plants cannot grow in, that is, water which is low in oxygen.

The great lily pad of the lotus plant provides shelter for the fish that swim under its pad. It also provides a place for frogs to sit and sun themselves. The lotus flower provides a nice drink of nectar for the butterflies and bees. The plant is quite splendid indeed. It provides so much out of so little.

Use the lotus as an analogy to relate to the young person's life.

Case study: **Child**

Eleven-year-old Bailey was referred for issues of depression. She was physically and sexually abused by her father and mother.

The clinician explains the Lotus tool to Bailey. Bailey is impressed by the story. She had no idea of any of this about the lotus. She states that she feels like she is—and has been for a long time—growing in the mud or maybe not even growing at all, but struggling. She feels that at times she blossoms but she is definitely not the large brilliant lotus plants from the photographs.

This was an initial opening up for the clinician and Bailey.

Case study: **Adolescent**

Sophia is a 16-year-old adolescent who was referred for depression and suicidal ideation.

The clinician explains the Lotus tool. Sophia states that she has always loved the lotus and it is her favorite flower. She states that she knows the history and has written a poem about it. Upon reading the poem, it is clear that Sophia is identifying the struggle of the lotus with her own struggles.

This was a wonderful opening up and gathering of information for the clinician and Sophia.

KEY TO OPEN THE HEART

Purpose

» To gather information about who and/or what allows the child or adolescent to feel like he or she is safe and at peace.

What you will need

» Old recycled keys in any kind of container

» Recycled construction paper

» Markers

Activity

Discuss what keys mean. What is their purpose? They are used to lock and unlock things.

Let the child or adolescent choose a key from the container to keep.

If we think about unlocking things like doors, we could also think about unlocking our hearts. Ask: "Who or what in your environment opens your heart?" Maybe it is a person with whom the child or adolescent feels comfortable. Maybe it is a special animal. Maybe it is even a stuffed toy. Maybe it is a place, such as a park or a church.

Brainstorm together some ideas of what these people or things could be, using the cues above to get started, and then have the child write down his answer on the construction paper.

Case study: **Child**

Nolan is a seven-year-old referred for issues of biting and hitting himself.

The clinician introduces Nolan to the Key to Open the Heart tool. Nolan chooses a key and together he and the clinician brainstorm ideas. Some of the ideas they jointly create are teddy bears, which feel especially comforting at night, grandparents, and more.

Nolan creates his list and he is surprised at what he finds. Two of Nolan's greatest comforts are his mother and his teacher. He reveals that sometimes he gets so frustrated and does not understand things. Sometimes the frustration is so severe that he bites or hits himself.

This is a wonderful opening up for the clinician and Nolan.

Case study: **Adolescent**

Avery is a 13-year-old adolescent who was referred for night terrors and bedwetting.

The clinician introduces Avery to the Key to Open the Heart tool. Avery understands and chooses a key from the recycled key jar. Avery and the clinician brainstorm many ideas. Avery creates her own list and it includes horseback riding, her riding instructor, and friends at the horse barn. Avery states that the barn is the place where she feels the most secure and, the moment she opens the barn door and walks in, she feels her heart calming and has a sense of general well-being. She states that she no longer feels that way at school or at home. Lately, she has not been doing well in school and her parents are very angry and have threatened her with having to give up her horseback riding and activities at the barn.

This was a wonderful opening up for Avery and the clinician.

PANDORA'S BOX

Purpose

> » To open up and explore the issues of concern currently on the child's or adolescent's mind.

What you will need

> » Large sheet of recycled cardboard or plastic
> » Large marker
> » Regular recycled paper

Activity

Discuss the idea of Pandora's Box.

Pandora and her box are mythical. In the fable of Pandora, when the box was opened, the evils of the world came out and only hope was left in the box. In our story, hope stays in the box and the negatives, worries and fears come out.

Brainstorm with the child or adolescent a few things that could come out of the box. Examples could be anger, fear, etc. Write these ideas on the large board.

Allow time for the child or adolescent to create her own list on paper. Discuss this list together.

Remember to share that hope is at the bottom of Pandora's Box.

Case study: **Child**

Haydon is a six-year-old girl who was referred due to the loss of her father and mother. Her father was incarcerated after her mother's death.

The clinician and Haydon talk about the Pandora's Box tool. Haydon is able to generate her own list. Haydon uses some words and creates many drawings. She demonstrates frustration and draws a picture of her mom going up to heaven.

This was a good opening for the clinician and Haydon to begin to work together.

Case study: **Adolescent**

Blake is a 16-year-old adolescent who was referred for threatening teachers and the high school principal.

The clinician introduces Blake to the concept of the Pandora's Box tool. Blake readily writes his own long list. It appears as though Blake does not see a future beyond gangs, drugs and even self-prostitution.

Blake was able to open up immediately—he just needed a tool. The clinician talks about the idea that, maybe now that they are together, they can create a plan where Blake could have hope. Blake concedes that maybe they could.

TIPS FOR CLINICIANS: Make sure to use and reinforce the idea of hope coming from Pandora's Box.

BIRD'S WING

Purpose

» To allow the child or adolescent to open up and discuss what would make him or her feel lighter and less stressed.

What you will need

» Only you

Activity

Discuss the idea of taking flight on a bird's wing. What would that look like and feel like? Would it be exhilarating? What would we have to let go of to feel lighter or more carefree?

Case study: **Child**

Aria is a five-year-old girl who was referred for symptoms of post-traumatic stress disorder. She is newly adopted out of the foster care system. Her siblings are still in foster care.

The clinician explains the idea of the Bird's Wing tool. Aria identifies with it and remembers a movie called "Rescuers," in which a mouse had a bird friend with whom he would fly and who would take him away from bad people.

Aria at age five remembers her bad early experiences at ages two and three. She states that if she could be like the mouse, she would go and pick up her siblings and bring them to her new home. Aria loves her new parents but she is very worried about her siblings.

This was a wonderful transition for Aria and the clinician to talk about the complex issues that Aria is facing.

Case study: **Adolescent**

Chase is a 15-year-old who was referred for symptoms of post-traumatic stress disorder. He was involved in a farming accident in which he lost his foot. He now has a prosthetic foot and is learning to work with it.

The clinician explains the Bird's Wing tool to Chase. Chase immediately identifies with it and states that if he could learn to use his prosthetic foot, he could get off the farm and get to really make something of his life. He would like to take flight on a bird's wing and get off the farm and sell it. He reports he is terrified of any farm equipment and does not want his family to be farming anymore.

This is a good opening for the clinician and Chase to explore Chase's complicated issues.

BIRTHDAY BALLOONS 2

Purpose

> » To identify who or what the child or adolescent would like to include more of in his or her life.

What you will need

> » A drawing of a balloon bouquet

Activity

Have the child or adolescent identify in each balloon who or what he would like to have more of in his life; in particular, at special times like birthdays.

Case study: **Child**

Penny is a five-year-old girl who was referred for issues of anxiety and possible reactive attachment disorder.

Penny understands the concept of the Birthday Balloons 2 tool. In her balloon, she draws a picture of her dad and her mom. She also draws two dogs. Penny reveals that she misses her mom and dad and states that they work a lot and she is now in five-year-old kindergarten. This is Penny's first time away from home. She would also like to have two dogs!

This is a lovely beginning for Penny to be able to readily identify what she is anxious about.

Case study: **Adolescent**

Rory is a 13-year-old who was referred for issues of underage drinking and drug use.

The clinician explains the Birthday Balloons 2 tool. Rory writes the following words in his balloons: "Mom," "Mom," "Mom," "Mom." Rory reveals that his mom is on probation for stealing. He wishes his mom could spend more time with him and was not getting into trouble "all of the time." This was a great beginning for Rory. He was quickly able to reveal a great deal of information surrounding his family life and his need for his mother.

REMEMBER WHEN?

Purpose

» To help children and adolescents identify positive times in their lives.

What you will need

» Large sheet of recycled cardboard
» Markers

Activity

Have the child or adolescent brainstorm events or times in her life when there have been fun or good times. Talk about them and highlight on the cardboard those good feelings and who or what was present at the time of these feelings.

Case study: **Child**

Kara is a seven-year-old girl who was referred for anxiety and depression. Her father passed away last year at this time.

The clinician shares with Kara the Remember When? tool. Kara does some brainstorming, remembering good events and feelings from the past. She also remembers recent fun experiences like going to the movies with her mom or playing with her sister. She also likes sleepovers and Grandma's home.

This is a good opening up, as Kara has good memories even from the recent past, which can be used to help her.

Case study: **Adolescent**

Gabriella is a 16-year-old who was referred for depression after being sexually abused by her brother.

The clinician introduces Gabriella to the Remember When? tool. Gabriella is able to brainstorm many fun times in her life and then she comes to the sexual abuse. She reveals that it is hard for her to think of future good times or even present good times since the event occurred.

This is a good initial opening for the clinician and Gabriella.

HEROES

Purpose

» To identify and gather information about whom the child or adolescent views as a role model or a hero.

What you will need

» One piece of recycled cardboard or plastic on which you have written the word "Heroes"

Activity

Share with the child or adolescent the sheet with the word "Heroes" written on it. Have the child or adolescent identify as many heroes as he can from the past as well as the present.

Case study: **Child**

Oliver is a six-year-old who was referred for ongoing separation anxiety issues.

The clinician introduces Oliver to the concept of the Heroes tool. Oliver understands and speaks instead of writing his heroes. The clinician records them on the sheet for him. His top heroes are his mom and dad, and his grandmother and grandfather.

Oliver reveals that he does not like to leave home and that he worries about his parents. He fears that something bad will happen to him when he is not present.

This is a good beginning for Oliver and the clinician.

Case study: **Adolescent**

Evelyn is a 14-year-old who was referred for issues of peer pressure, body image and stress.

The clinician introduces Evelyn to the concept of the Heroes tool. Evelyn struggles with listing current heroes. She states that when she was in middle school and grammar school, her parents were her heroes, but now that she is in high school, things have changed. She is not sure who her hero is. She likes some of the pop icons, but isn't sure they are her heroes.

The clinician and Evelyn talk about the change from her parents as heroes to being uncertain of who is her hero.

This was a good information gathering for the clinician and Evelyn.

ALLIES

Purpose

» To identify and gather information on who the child or adolescent feels is an ally in life.

What you will need

» A piece of cardboard or plastic titled "Allies"

Activity

Share with the child or adolescent what the term "ally" means. Explain than an ally is someone who is supportive, or "on your side."

Ask the child or adolescent to list all of her current allies.

Case study: **Child**

Diamond is an 11-year-old who was referred for body image and beginning eating disorder issues.

The clinician presents the Allies tool to Diamond. She creates a list of mostly friends and also a website. The clinician learns that Diamond does not trust her parents. She feels like they are lying to her. They tell her she is beautiful and that her body is changing into a woman but she feels ugly and fat.

She believes her allies are the other girls in school who share similar feelings, as well as a website where girls can join a forum to talk about dieting.

This was a crucial gathering of information for Diamond and the clinician.

Case study: **Adolescent**

Silas is a 16-year-old who was referred for chronic marijuana use.

Silas is introduced to the concept of the Allies tool. He creates a list of allies. Among them are his father and brother. Silas reveals that his father and brother both smoke marijuana and do not feel this is a problem for them or Silas.

This, again, was a crucial gathering of information for the clinician and Silas.

KITES

Purpose

» To determine what the child or adolescent needs in order to feel as though he or she can fly free or be without the burden of what brought the child or adolescent in for help.

What you will need

» A kite—you can make this out of used Popsicle sticks, string and tissue paper

» A small kite for the child or adolescent to take home (if you choose)

Activity

Show the child or adolescent the kite. Ask him if he ever remembers flying a kite. What did it feel like to get the kite up and flying? What did it feel like while the kite was flying high?

Give the child or adolescent a small kite to take home and have fun.

Case study: **Child**

Preston is a six-year-old who was referred for attention deficit hyperactivity disorder (ADHD) and hitting himself.

The clinician introduces Preston to the Kites tool. She shows Preston her kite and lets him handle it. He likes the colors and the shape of the dragon. Preston remembers flying a kite with his dad for the first time last year. Preston states that it was fun, and he loved it when he would run with the kite and then suddenly it would start to fly, almost like magic! He also states that when it was up and flying in the sky and he was running faster and faster with the string, it was exciting but also a little scary because the kite almost got caught in a tree. His dad swore when that happened.

The clinician introduces Preston to the analogy of working hard to get the kite to fly and, then once it is flying, things can get easier. She asks Preston if he is willing to work to find alternative ways of behaving so that he does not hit himself. Preston agrees to work together and also work on ways of coping with the newly diagnosed ADHD.

The clinician gives Preston the small kite to take home for fun and reinforcement.

This was a good information-gathering meeting.

Case study: **Adolescent**

Katherine is a 17-year-old adolescent who was referred for alcohol or other drug abuse (AODA) issues and possible oppositional defiant disorder.

The clinician meets with Katherine and introduces her to the Kites tool. Initially, Katherine laughs, but she is interested in the large dragon kite, which the clinician lets her look at and hold.

Katherine reveals that she never went kite flying with her parents. Both of her parents are working professionals and she is the only child. She reveals that many times she was home alone or "pawned off" on a babysitter. What she remembers from her childhood is mostly watching TV. She states it wasn't until she had a car, which was on her 16th birthday, that she actually was able to see her friends regularly unless their parents drove.

Katherine revealed much anger and bitterness. This was a good opening tool.

NEW CHAPTER

Purpose

- » To identify ways of moving forward with a new activity, plan or behavior.

What you will need

- » Small chapter books
- » Large chapter books

Activity

Discuss what a chapter means. It is another part of the story. Ask the child or adolescent to identify what other parts of his life story he would like to explore or move on to. Reinforce that he gets to identify and choose what to work on first.

Case study: **Child**

Jasmine is a nine-year-old who was referred for anxiety with panic attacks.

The clinician introduces Jasmine to the New Chapter tool. Jasmine is able to draw the analogy of her life compared with a book. She reveals that she is stuck in one chapter and she begins to cry. She can't stop feeling scared or worried or having physical sensations of trembling.

This was a good gathering of information for the clinician and Jasmine.

Case study: **Adolescent**

Calvin is a 13-year-old boy who was referred for cyber-addiction and underage drinking.

The clinician introduces Calvin to the New Chapter tool. Calvin understands the analogy, and also understands that his parents and teachers would like him to "start a new chapter," but he isn't sure he wants to for the cyber-addiction. He admits that he knows he has to stop the drinking, but he reveals that he likes both.

This was a great gathering of information for the clinician and Calvin.

MY FAMILY/MY CAREGIVERS

Purpose

» To discover whom the child or adolescent identifies as people who take care of him or her on a regular basis; in addition, we will be identifying whom the child or adolescent trusts.

What you will need

» Photo of a tree, such as a bonsai tree, or any depiction of a tree, including one that might be visible through the window

Activity

Talk with the child or adolescent about the idea that trees have many branches. Look at the form of the trees in the pictures or through the window.

Discuss the idea that different branches represent different people who help the child or adolescent on a day-to-day basis.

Case study: **Child**

Abigail is a ten-year-old child who was referred for sadness, anxiety and racing thoughts.

The clinician introduces Abigail to the My Family/My Caregivers tool. Abigail is readily able to identify a number of people who care for her, including her mom, her dad, her two grandmothers (both of whom live with Abigail), her sisters, an aunt and a family friend who has been coming over more and more often.

Abigail reveals that her primary caregivers, Mom and Dad, have not been available as much lately as "something is wrong" with her grandmother. She is not able to identify what is wrong and she feels as though she is the only person in the family who doesn't know. Abigail reveals that she thinks maybe her grandmother is dying.

This was an incredible information gathering for the clinician and Abigail.

Case study: **Adolescent**

Jonathan is a 17-year-old adolescent who was referred for depression and suicidal ideation. He was recently mandated to begin alcohol and other drug abuse (AODA) treatment after his school randomly drug-tested him and he came up positive for THC (the principal psychoactive constituent of cannabis) and opioids.

The clinician introduces Jonathan to the My Family/My Caregivers tool. Jonathan reveals that, for most of his life, he has not had a consistent family. His parents divorced when he was seven, and ever since then, he has not visited his father's side of the family. As time passed, his father stopped visiting, and he also was unable to see some of his cousins with whom he was very close. In the meantime, he has experienced other male role models—his grandfather, who currently lives in another country, and his mother's two boyfriends. Jonathan does not like either boyfriend and states that when his mother is with them she behaves differently and drinks more. Now, his mother is just drinking all of the time. Jonathan feels like he has no one to go to or talk with. He has started to self-medicate.

This was a wonderful opening up for both Jonathan and the clinician.

EPILOGUE

Dear reader, take a breath with me and take heart. The children and adolescents with whom we work, as well as those whom you have read about in the case samples, often are troubled and sad. However, these children and adolescents—as well as their families—benefited greatly from counseling: They felt better and their lives became better.

We can do this together. Learn from the children and adolescents that you work with—let them lead you and take you, too, to new ideas, concepts and tools that *you* create to help them. Be bold. Be brave—after all, they are!

With much peace and hope,

Yours in camaraderie,

Dawn